PRAISE FOR THE BOOK BABES AND
Between the Covers:

"I wouldn't normally and publicly praise a book I'm in, but in the case of these enthusiastic readers who devour books as if they were gorgeous and smart lovers, I'm making an exception. Any reader will be swept away by this swift and useful guide through life's dilemmas through literature. These two guides have read deeply and widely and their sure touch translates into practical and pleasurable uses for books. Trust them, they'll fix you right up, and they are cheaper than shrinks."

—ANDREI CODRESCU,
author of *New Orleans, Mon Amour: Twenty Years of Writing from the City* and *Jealous Witness: New Poems*

"Between the covers, the Book Babes are novel lovers."

—WHITNEY OTTO,
author of *How to Make an American Quilt*

"The Book Babes are brainy, funny, on the money. They're fantastic role models, showing young women that there's nothing sexier than someone who is well-read and witty."

—SUSAN SHAPIRO,
author of *Five Men Who Broke My Heart*

"The Book Babes' vast knowledge of books and their sometimes offbeat, always on-target judgments about quality literature are demonstrated in *Between the Covers*. I cannot imagine a more interesting, useful, and wise guide to literature—for women and men."

—STEVE WEINBERG,
author of *Taking on the Trust: The Epic Battle of Ida Tarbell and John D. Rockefeller*

"Margo Hammond and Ellen Heltzel are true goddesses of the literary world. And their love of the written word has been channeled into this fabulous volume—which contains a smorgasbord of book advice for every stage of a woman's life. Between the Covers should be required reading for 'book babes' everywhere (and I'm not just saying that because my book is listed herein)!"

—JANE GANAHL,
author of *Naked on the Page*

Between the Covers

About the Authors

Margo Hammond, former book editor for the *St. Petersburg Times,* has served as a National Book Critics Circle board member and as president of the Southern Book Critics Circle. She wrote a weekly travel column for *The New York Times* Syndicate and worked at *The Atlantic Monthly,* the *Washington Star,* and the *Baltimore Sun.* She lives in St. Petersburg, Florida.

Ellen Heltzel was features and book editor at *The Oregonian.* She serves on the National Book Critics Circle board and writes for a host of publications, including *The Washington Post, USA Today,* the *Chicago Tribune,* and *The Seattle Times.* She lives in Portland, Oregon.

As **The Book Babes**, Hammond and Heltzel have written a weekly column for Poynter Online and The Book Standard and a monthly column for *Good Housekeeping* magazine online. Their radio program airs monthly on WMNF-FM in Tampa, and their work has appeared in magazines and newspapers across the country. Visit them at **www.thebookbabes.com**, and send them your favorite book picks at **thebookbabes@yahoo.com**.

BETWEEN THE COVERS

The Book Babes' Guide to a Woman's Reading Pleasures

Margo Hammond

Ellen Heltzel

Da Capo Press

A Member of the Perseus Books Group

Designed by Brent Wilcox
Set in 11.5 point Berkeley Book by the Perseus Books Group

Library of Congress Cataloging-in-Publication Data
Hammond, Margo, 1949-
    Between the covers : the Book Babes' guide to a woman's reading pleasures / Margo Hammond and Ellen Heltzel.—1st Da Capo Press ed.
        p.   cm.
    Includes index.
    ISBN 978-0-7382-1229-6 (alk. paper)
    1. Women—Books and reading.   2. Women in literature.   I. Heltzel, Ellen.   II. Title.
    Z1039.W65H36 2008
    028'.9082—dc22

                                                                                            2008028385

First Da Capo Press edition 2008
Published by Da Capo Press
A Member of the Perseus Books Group
www.dacapopress.com

Da Capo Press books are available at special discounts for bulk purchases in the United States by corporations, institutions, and other organizations. For more information, please contact the Special Markets Department at the Perseus Books Group, 2300 Chestnut Street, Suite 200, Philadelphia, PA 19103, or call (800) 810-4145, ext. 5000, or e-mail special.markets@perseusbooks.com.

10 9 8 7 6 5 4 3 2 1

To Carl and Tim

Contents

V   Love, Sex, & Second Chances   119

VI   Home, Work, & Taking Care   145

VII   Babes in the World   197

VIII   Babes Without Borders   231

INTRODUCTION

"I have always imagined that Paradise
will be a kind of library."

JORGE LUIS BORGES

For book lovers, Paradise means getting between the covers. It means curling up with a good book, or finding just the right one on a bookstore or library shelf, or sharing a favorite with a friend.

And it's never been easier: There are now more books in circulation than ever before. Millions, to be imprecise—because precision would be impossible with today's biblio birth rate. This embarrassment of riches creates a quandary for the passionate reader: How do you wrap your mind around all the options?

We have an idea.

Just as the Dewey Decimal System was invented to impose order on books, we've created a system of our own to guide and stimulate your reading. It's hardly the equivalent of the time-honored catalogue. But it can help you in a way that Dewey cannot, because it follows the rhythms of a woman's life.

Make that a busy, curious woman, and one who likes to read. If you see yourself in this description, please come aboard. As the Book Babes, two book critics who have built a friendship and partnership around our enthusiasm for reading, our goal is to connect the dots between literature and your life.

For us, reading is as familiar and essential a habit as our morning coffee. It's an interactive sport that we practice every day, when our experience meets the author's words and transforms them.

Between the Covers is interactive, too. It revolves around lists—fifty-five in all, each including ten books that relate to the same theme, each approaching the theme in a different way. We start with some favorite women we've found through books. No saints here: Instead, they're individuals—from fiction and reality—who have gained dimension on the page. Their wit, intelligence, perseverance, and elegance remind us of qualities we want to foster in ourselves.

Then we get personal, dealing with how you feel about your looks and weight, your spiritual and artistic growth. Then come family matters, love life, attitudes about home and work. As the circle widens, we expand to your concern for the world at large. Finally, it's time to put up your feet and relax: Be an armchair traveler, a crime solver, a member of royalty.

In order to cover this range and reflect how women really read, our picks come from every corner. About a third are fiction (with a little poetry for good measure). A third are general nonfiction. The rest? Memoirs. This high proportion is no surprise: So many good memoirs have been published in the past fifteen years. And because this is a book about women and what we care about, personal stories take pride of place.

In our focus on women's lives today, we give priority to living authors and more recently published books. Not that we're against the classics, and a couple are tucked in where you might not expect them. But as much as we admire *Middlemarch* and *Anna Karenina,* our aim here is to showcase the tremendous variety and superb writing that's being created now.

Within this contemporary frame, we cast wide, reflecting the eclectic tastes of the truly passionate reader. You'll find literary fiction and chick lit. Mystery and self-help. Obscure books and best sellers.

If some of your favorites are missing, rest assured, some of ours are, too. This book isn't intended to circumscribe your reading, but to open it up and spur a wider search. Like a box of assorted chocolates, this selection gives you many ways to indulge.

While writing this book, we discovered what kinship books have. They echo or amplify each other, or take an opposing view. It's seven degrees of separation, literary-style. After reading Anchee Min's novel *Empress Orchid*, about the last empress of China, we picked up Alberto Manguel's *The Library at Night*, and it was as if the two books were talking to each other, and we were listening in. Describing his library in the French countryside, Manguel compared it to "the strange Chinese villa that in 1888 the capricious Empress Cixi caused to be built in the shape of a ship. . . ." A picture of her strange, land-bound ark cemented the image of the wily queen that Min already had placed in our minds. Discovering her for a second time, she was locked there forever, like John Keats's lovers on that Grecian urn.

More connections: In her novel *The Collection*, Gioia Diliberto imagines a young seamstress working in Coco Chanel's Paris atelier. In *My Mother's Wedding Dress*, Justine Picardie gives us an actual tour of the same workspace.

In *Going Gray: What I Learned About Beauty, Sex, Work, Motherhood, Authenticity, and Everything Else That Really Matters*, Anne Kreamer begins with a photograph from a trip that changed her life and her attitudes toward aging. One of the women in the photo is Akiko Busch, author of *Nine Ways to Cross a River*—another book that ruminates on the passage of time.

In *The Naked Woman: A Study of the Female Body*, Desmond Morris describes how women whitened their cheeks and blackened their teeth in ancient Japan, a beauty ritual that's described in Liza Dalby's novel, *The Tale of Murasaki*—itself inspired by the eleventh-century classic *The Tale of Genji*.

In making the choices for this book, one goal was to include as many of our unsung heroes as we could. Another was to come at well-known authors in fresh ways. Much as we love Ann Patchett's novels, she's represented here by her memoir *Truth & Beauty: A Friendship,* about her strange but loving relationship with a fellow poet and writer. (A novel by her mom, Jeanne Ray, did make our cut.) Mary Gordon's memoir *Circling My Mother* was picked over her better-known *Shadow Man*, a book about her father. Sara Gruen is featured not for her best-selling *Water for Elephants* but for *Riding Lessons*, another novel that similarly shows her devotion to animals.

In order to include as many favorites as we could, we mention only a few authors more than once. But please don't try this at home: If you like the book we recommend, that's the perfect reason to read more of what that author has written. Seek out the writers who teach or provoke or comfort you, and ask yourself why they do. Your answer matters, because what you read signals what you want to know and care about.

Between the Covers grows out of a long-distance collaboration that began after we met, appropriately enough, at a book convention during the 1990s. Both of us were book editors for newspapers—Margo in St. Petersburg, Florida, Ellen in Portland, Oregon. We kept in touch by phone and then the Internet, which led us to blogging before most people (including us!) had heard the term. Our back-and-forth discussions evolved into columns and recommendation lists that have appeared on various websites and in newspapers around the country.

What makes our collaboration work is not that our tastes in reading are the same, but that they complement each other. So, too, our lives: Ellen, a native Oregonian, has been married for more than thirty years and has two sons. Margo has been divorced and is remarried. A Wisconsin native, she has lived and worked in various cities in Europe and along the East Coast.

As with books, our political and religious views aren't the same, but we love to discuss them. Our differences contribute to a stimulating dialogue that's fueled by—yes, you guessed it—our love for reading. Book lovers are an informed, dissenting lot, so you may take issue with some of our choices. We welcome a different opinion. If there's ever peace on Earth, we think it will start when guns are replaced with books, when the thirst for knowledge will outpace the quest for power.

The cue for our reading habits and this book can be found in Ralph Waldo Emerson, who observed, "What lies behind us and what lies before us are small matters compared to what lies within us."

No, the Babes can't guarantee that reading makes you a better person. But it can make you a deeper one: a smarter, more interesting, more imaginative woman who carries that knowledge and understanding into the world.

So, welcome to our divine library. We look forward to introducing you to some old friends and some new ones. Some may merely interest you. Others may change your life.

I

BABES WE LOVE

Women have written poetry, trekked across continents, and ruled empires. But for most of human history, it was his story: men casting themselves as the heroes of their own sagas. Women were left to whisper their stories to each other—in red tents where they were isolated during menstrual cycles, next to each other in the fields, in churches and factories, over backyard fences, and at beauty parlors.

In the 1970s, artist Judy Chicago decided to give a shout-out to the forgotten women of myth and history. As the women's movement gathered steam, she created an unusual art installation: thirty-nine place settings, each dedicated to a different female figure, set on a triangle-shaped table. The settings featured ceramic plates decorated with a stylized version of a vulva. On the floor below porcelain tiles were inscribed with the names of 999 more notable women. Chicago called her ensemble *The Dinner Party*.

When the party was first exhibited in 1979, many viewers could scarcely see the forest for the vagina. In the ensuing uproar, Chicago made her point: Women deserve a place at the table.

Inspired by Chicago's tribute, the Book Babes imagine an all-woman celebration of their own. Ours is composed of thirty-two extraordinary women we met in the pages of thirty biographies, memoirs, and novels (four of our guests come as couples—lesbians living on the rue de Fleurus in Paris and a pair of bisexual anthropologists). They speak to us in different ways—through fiction, biography, and memoir—but their stories come together to offer testimony about their lives.

Like the figures honored by Chicago, these women who've been invited to feast with us are achievers—but not always in the traditional sense. Heroic exploits aren't the only reason to celebrate a life. Some of them are trailblazers. Others are "originals," with their own special sense of style. Still others are iconoclasts. More important, they're thirty-two high-spirited, smart, ass-kickin' women whose stories can inspire us all.

Writing down their lives—and drawing attention to themselves—has not always come easy for women. The ancient Greek poet Sappho wrote verses about her love life. Lady Murasaki drew on her own experiences to re-create Japanese court life in *The Tale of Genji* (considered the world's first novel). But most women writers, contrary to the archetype of the lone male embarking on his journey of discovery, didn't play the starring role in their own work. This is especially evident in the autobiographical writings that came out of European convents during the Middle Ages, when nuns wrote about their relationship to the divine. In *The Life of St. Teresa by Herself,* the sixteenth-century Spanish mystic from Avila warns you to "pay not attention to the intellect, which is merely being tiresome." Instead, give yourself to God.

As religious writings gave way to more secular ones, the family replaced God as the focal point of women's memoirs. Personal stories took on importance only in relationship to other family members. Even the captive narratives written by white European women kidnapped by Native Americans and the accounts of freed female slaves spoke to a purpose greater than the individual experience—the former to bolster the religious faith of the colonizers, the latter to create sympathy for the abolitionist cause.

Gradually that has changed. Now all the literary forms that deal with the universals in human experience—the quest, the romance, the odyssey, the tragic or comic mode—are available to women, says Jill Ker Conway in *When Memory Speaks*. But even as women have stepped up to center stage in their memoirs, they often still keep sight of their roots, producing more textured stories in the process.

Conway is a good illustration. In her first memoir, *The Road from Coorain,* she describes her hardscrabble childhood on her family's sheep farm in the Australian Outback. Her follow-up, *True North,* begins with her emigration to America in 1960 and ends with her appointment as the first woman president of the all-women's Smith College in 1975. In both cases, as her personal history unfolds, so does the warp and woof of the society in which she operated.

"We travel through life guided by an inner life plot," says Conway. That plot is created by our family and societal norms, but also by our insights into ourselves and the universe around us. It is the sum of all those parts that has made the lives of women in this section so engaging—and why we'd fight to be seated next to any one of them at a dinner party.

THAT SAY, "I DID IT MY WAY"

1. *The Woman Warrior* by Maxine Hong Kingston. Few women can write their own story, capture the yin of an entire cultural legacy, and defy it at the same time. But Kingston is up to the multitask in this memoir, as she expunges the sorrows and sexism that are part of her Chinese heritage. A self-proclaimed "woman warrior," she resists the "American-feminine" of her immigrant upbringing and claims an assertive voice. Furious at a meeker classmate's silence, she pulls the girl's hair and yells, "Talk! Talk!"

2. *Reading Lolita in Tehran* by Azar Nafisi. Nafisi, a teacher in Tehran, and seven of her best women students defied Iran's ayatollahs with the weapon repressive regimes fear most: reading. Meeting secretly at Nafisi's apartment every Thursday morning for two years, they shed their robes, scarves, and inhibitions to discuss forbidden classics by Vladimir Nabokov, F. Scott Fitzgerald, Henry James, and Jane Austen. The group relates most to *Lolita,* the story of a young girl kept captive by someone else's fantasy. It's not that big a leap from a controlling dirty old man to the thought police.

3. *My Life So Far* by Jane Fonda. Dividing her narrative into three acts as if she were starring in her own play, Fonda describes her many roles: daughter of a beloved actor who was an emotionally distant father, wife to three oversized egos, workout guru, and political activist. By Act Three, appropriately titled "Beginning," she is simply Jane, alone but finally not lonely. Nothing is off-limits: her mother's suicide, her controversial trip to Hanoi, her bulimia. If you don't weep at her dying father's silent tears, you probably sat dry-eyed through *On Golden Pond*.

4. *Dust Tracks on a Road* by Zora Neale Hurston. In the 1920s and '30s, black male authors rejected her use of rural patois. White publishers censored her. No wonder Hurston's work was ignored for nearly three decades. Now her novels, folklore studies, and this inventive memoir about growing up in "burly, boiling" black Florida are back with a vengeance. She died penniless, but she left words rich with empathy for poor rural folk: "You, who play zig-zag lightning of power over the world, with the grumbling thunder in your wake, think kindly of those who walk in the dust."

5. *The Bone People* by Keri Hulme. An odd trio inhabits this lonely, lyrical novel set against a remote New Zealand backdrop. The reclusive painter Kerewin befriends a small boy, Simon, and through him another loner, the child's foster father, Joe. Past pain defines their individual lives and invades their relationship in a story that Hulme flavors with Maori phrases and the tempestuous roar of the sea. The Romantic poets meet one tough and independent woman: "Whatever you want of me, I will give," Joe tells Kerewin. "Even absence?" she counters.

6. *Secrets of the Flesh: A Life of Colette* by Judith Thurman. Funny thing about the French writer Colette: No matter where you look in her long life, she seems both sinner and saint. So you don't need to wonder why, after she died in 1954, she was the first woman to receive a state funeral in France—and was also denied a Christian burial. Thurman portrays a scrappy survivor who went topless at a time when proper women didn't show their ankles. You'll like her pluck, but not her back-stabbing.

7. *Little Women* by Louisa May Alcott. Family values and a surprisingly independent main character burnish this nineteenth-century classic. Jo March, of course, is a stand-in for the author, who turns her alter ego into a bright and impulsively kind girl who "valued goodness highly" but also treasured the life of the mind. She treats the lives of her sisters Meg, Beth, and Amy as no less important than her own. And she marries not for money, but for love. Cynics can regard Jo's rose-colored vision as pure fiction, but millions have embraced the idea that ambition and self-sacrifice can come in the same package.

8. *Frida Kahlo: The Paintings* by Hayden Herrera. Herrera's 1983 bio still is the most complete picture of Kahlo you'll find. But the art historian was smart to follow up with this collection, where you can absorb her cogent commentary while looking at the Mexican painter's work. Kahlo began painting after a horrific traffic accident at eighteen shattered her body for life. Now her paintings sell for millions—a fact that probably would amuse and infuriate the flamboyant iconoclast who was always scrambling for "dough." But she'd love Herrera's description of her mind-jarring work.

9. *Two Lives: Gertrude and Alice* by Janet Malcolm. Like Kahlo, Gertrude Stein and Alice B. Toklas have been turned into pop icons, but only as a matched set. Gertrude, who blew off her own brother when he didn't honor her genius, wanted to be center stage, but not Alice, who was born to serve. The book is built around the riddle of how two Jewish lesbians escaped deportation in Nazi-occupied France. Yet Malcolm's look at Gertrude's art and the power balance between Gertie and Alice makes you think about how any couple divides up the pie.

10. *Mae West: It Ain't No Sin* by Simon Louvish. Before *Sex and the City,* before Madonna, there was West, the sexy woman who made fun of sex. Usually tightly corseted, and always loose with the innuendo, the bawdy entertainer may have become a caricature of herself, but she was one of the first to show us how to be a babe with brains. Thankfully, this bio focuses on her anatomy above the neck. Forget those rumors of secret lovers—Mae West was too busy perfecting her scripts.

THAT BLAZED A TRAIL

1. *I Should Be Extremely Happy in Your Company: A Novel of Lewis and Clark* by Brian Hall. In this fictional retelling of the Lewis and Clark expedition, the Indian guide speaks to the reader in broken English. But don't let that fool you. Sacagawea is a kingpin—hey, why not queenpin?—who holds the trek together at a crucial moment. Kidnapped by another tribe as a girl, the nation's most famous woman trailblazer knew the language and terrain to get "big knife" and "red hair" through a scary patch. When she describes her reunion with a Shoshone brother, her words will melt your heart.

2. *Desert Queen: The Extraordinary Life of Gertrude Bell: Adventurer, Adviser to Kings, Ally of Lawrence of Arabia* by Janet Wallach. Talk about a woman with attitude. Raised in the Victorian age, the willful, red-haired Bell defied custom to attend Oxford and become a self-styled roving ambassador. She was the only woman at the 1921 conference that redrew the map of the Middle East and created modern Iraq. Read her story—and this is the best-told version—for a better grip on history and how good intentions don't always produce good results.

3. *I Was Amelia Earhart* by Jane Mendelsohn. What happened after Earhart's plane disappeared over the Pacific in 1937? Here's one theory that stokes our ongoing romance with the mysterious flyer who "wore leather and silk with such glamorous nonchalance": The record-breaking aviatrix and her male navigator became "between voyagers" (a phrase borrowed from the Tibetan Book of the Dead). In this gauzy, feel-good novel, you get not only life after death, but love after death.

4. *Intertwined Lives: Margaret Mead, Ruth Benedict, and Their Circle* by Lois W. Banner. Your head will spin faster than Linda Blair's as you read this twofer bio about these bisexual anthropologists. Not to worry: Banner's coupling of the two women, who had conventional marriages while also becoming intimate friends, gives context and a lesson on how their free-love mindsets affected what they thought they saw in the field. Step beyond the partner swapping, and you see two independent thinkers who fought the tide of taboo with their questions about sexual identity.

5. *Reason for Hope: A Spiritual Journey* by Jane Goodall with Phillip Berman. If you think all scientists are atheists, primatologist Goodall will prove you wrong. In this memoir, written with an expert on comparative religions, she talks about mystical experiences, her surprising discoveries in Tanzania, the risk of environmental destruction, and the religious faith of her grandmother and mother. When she describes lying on the forest floor to watch chimp David Greybeard feeding on figs, it's pure poetry.

6. *Lazy B: Growing Up on a Cattle Ranch in the American Southwest* by Sandra Day O'Connor and H. Alan Day. The first woman to be appointed to the Supreme Court came a long way, baby, from her rugged upbringing in sagebrush country. Her roots are recalled in text and black-and-white photos that underscore the tough, macho culture into which she was born. This may have braced her for the sexism ahead: After her 1952 graduation from Stanford Law School, she was offered a legal secretary job. O'Connor didn't rewrite the rules, but she tweaked them, "wearing my bra and my wedding ring" all the way to the top.

7. *The Tale of Murasaki: A Novel* by Liza Dalby. An eleventh-century noblewoman named Murasaki wrote the world's first novel, *The Tale of Genji*, a thousand-page-plus doorstop. Too daunting?

Dalby's fanciful creation of Murasaki's memoirs conjures the same exotic world of white-powdered faces, blackened teeth, and court jealousies—in far fewer pages. A scholar of Japanese culture, Dalby includes the real Murasaki's lyrical but opaque poems, which suggest liaisons with women friends, a marriage and, of course, a writer's angst.

8. *Barbara Jordan: An American Hero* by Mary Beth Rogers. Whether she was bellowing from the podium like an Old Testament prophet or hauling herself around in a wheelchair, the first black woman elected to the U.S. Congress from the South changed our view of what a politician was supposed to look and sound like. But contrary to the usual political bio, this is not a puff job. Easily bored and impatient, Jordan was a stubborn fighter who was fiercely patriotic, says Rogers. Large like her home state of Texas, Jordan called herself "an unhyphenated American"—our kind of hero.

9. *The Stone Diaries* by Carol Shields. The fictional Daisy Good-will Flett is no Betty Friedan, but that's precisely Shields's point: Her life as wife, mother, and self-discoverer turns her into an accidental pioneer over the course of the twentieth century—a time of profound change in women's status. Canadian author Shields won a Pulitzer Prize, and deservedly so, for portraying Flett's life from start to finish, revealing not only the transformation but also the psychological needs to which that change responded.

10. *Insecure at Last: A Political Memoir* by Eve Ensler. If you've ever seen *The Vagina Monologues*—and we recommend you do— you would expect its creator to tell her own story this way. Her father's physical abuse when she was a child set the stage for her work as a playwright, but other women's lives have informed it, too. She has logged untold miles to witness the horrific violence against women and turned her personal pain into activism, raising buckets of cash to stop it. Agree or not with her political views, you'll be moved to tears by the sad stories and her own search for release.

WITH SIGNATURE STYLE

1. *My Life in France* by Julia Child with Alex Prud'homme. A raspy voice trilling "Bon appetit!" permeates Julia Child's delicious memoir, written with her grandnephew and published posthumously. "Woe!" she laments after failing her first exam at Le Cordon Bleu. "Yuck," she says of a ladies' lunch in Oslo, where her diplomat husband is posted. "Hooray," she declares after landing a contract for *Mastering the Art of French Cooking*. She serves up her gastronomical journey from a childhood of overcooked lamb to feasts of oysters and foie gras with just the right balance of bite and humility.

2. *Edith Wharton* by Hermione Lee. Once out of favor, Wharton has returned to join America's literary pantheon. Born into money and society, she capitalized on those perks to write enduring fiction that dissected her class. At a time when wealth was isolated in clumps (no income tax!), she started by writing about houses and landscaping, noting that "nothing adds more to the charm of a drawing-room than a well-decorated bookcase." Yes, she could be snooty and high-handed. But kudos to her for penetrating the inner lives of the rich and wannabes, and for not letting creature comforts define her life.

3. *Emma* by Jane Austen. We'd be "clueless" (remember the movie modeled on this plot?) if we didn't include a Jane Austen character in our list of women with style, and Emma wins the vote. Even if you can see her foibles as well as the plot unfolding from the get-go, Emma's spirited optimism and belief in herself make her a timeless and uplifting example of one young woman pushing against the headwinds of a hidebound society. Emma is a change agent with a smile, crusading for the best of all causes—love.

4. *Mistress of Modernism: The Life of Peggy Guggenheim* by Mary V. Dearborn. Too bad most people remember the "silly oversized sunglasses" Peggy sported late in life and the famous men she bedded, says biographer Dearborn. There's so much more to celebrate about this stylishly bohemian heiress. Her Uncle Solomon, of Guggenheim Museum fame, disapproved of women collectors, and yet her financial support of artists—yes, many did become her lovers—changed the course of modern art. Says novelist Gore Vidal, she was like the last of Henry James's trans-Atlantic heroines, Daisy Miller, "with rather more balls."

5. *Confessions of a Teen Sleuth* by Chelsea Cain. If there's any substitute for reading the Nancy Drew series in rerun, this parody of everybody's favorite girl detective is the one. It's pure fun built on

JACKIE, THE BOOK

Dozens of books have been written about Jacqueline Kennedy Onassis. None of them are very good.

What Jackie Taught Us: Lessons from the Remarkable Life of Jacqueline Kennedy Onassis by Tina Santi Flaherty, is too adoring. Kitty Kelley's *Jackie Oh!* is shamelessly gossipy. Donald Spoto's biography *Jacqueline Bouvier Kennedy Onassis: A Life* is well-researched but bloodless. In *Farewell Jackie: A Portrait of Her Final Days*, Edward Klein managed to strip away some of the myths about this very private woman (the book opens with a picture that shows a cigarette dangling from her lips), but his reliance on anonymous sources and tips from the nurse and doorman cheapens the effort. Even fictional versions can't get it right—just look at *The Secret Memoirs of Jacqueline Kennedy Onassis* by Ruth Francisco and *Jack's Widow* by Eve Pollard, two trashy novels based on the former First Lady's life.

Why has it been so hard to write something of quality about this iconic figure?

I've adored Jackie, as so many of us insist on calling her, ever since I was eleven and found out she wore a size 10 shoe. With feet that measured $9^{1}/_{2}$, I felt I could at last stand up, so to speak, to all those tactless salesmen who chortled when they measured me for shoes.

Maybe my obsession with Jackie's shoe size holds the key to why it's so hard for any one book to size her up. She was bigger than life: Stylish First Lady. America's Queen. Gracious Hostess. Grieving Widow. Clothes Horse. Horsewoman. Cuckolded Wife. Protective Mom. Culture Maven. Book Lover. Manhattan Matron. In sum, a woman who had big shoes to fill, and knew how to fill them.

~ Margo

the idea that the series author, Carolyn Keene, is actually Nancy's college roommate. Fed up with the way Carolyn is borrowing her name and exploits for her books, the impeccably coiffed and dressed Nancy steps forward with a karate chop or two and solves such lingering mysteries as what happened to her mother. (In the original series, Mom died when Nancy was young; in this spoof, she has a whole other life beyond River Heights.)

6. *Me: Stories of My Life* by Katharine Hepburn. Hepburn's un-polished stories of family, lovers, and the "pictures" she made feed into Kate's carefully cultivated image of herself as a pants-wearing, pigheaded free spirit. William J. Mann's *Kate: The Woman Who Was Hepburn* tries to shatter such mythmaking, but Kate's own version is more fun. Check out page 389: "Now I'm going to tell you about Spencer. You may think you've waited a long time. But let's face it, so did I. I was thirty-three."

7. *Longing* by J. D. Landis. Janice Galloway wrote another good novel about pianist Clara Schumann, which is simply called *Clara*. But for its wit and tempo we prefer this variation on a theme, a fictionalized version of the nineteenth-century's most famous woman musician and her composer spouse, Robert. Landis portrays the controlling father, genius husband, and their famous friends. After Robert went to the funny farm, Clara brought home the bacon and cooked enough to serve their seven children (the eighth died as an infant). And she still had time left over to dally with Brahms.

8. *If You Can't Be Free, Be a Mystery: In Search of Billie Holiday* by Farah Jasmine Griffin. You remember her signature gardenia, drug addiction, and "burned voice," says Griffin in this free-ranging riff. But Billie Holiday was not just a tragic figure who stood onstage and sung her woes. You don't have to be drugged out or crazy to be creative. Just the opposite. What gets lost in most accounts of Holiday's life is the musical genius of the woman Ella Fitzgerald called "the first modern singer." Griffin corrects the record.

9. *Even Cowgirls Get the Blues* by Tom Robbins. Sissy Hankshaw, the star of Robbins's wise and extravagant 1976 novel, burst on the scene just as American women were finding stronger voices. The perfect role model for those who fear their gender is an impediment to success, Sissy shows how any handicap—even two over-size thumbs—can be turned into an opportunity. She uses "those bananas, those sausages, those nightsticks, those pinkish pods" to become the world's best hitchhiker. Talk about making lemonade out of lemons, or in this case, turning "ruddy zucchini" into symbols of self-expression that still resonate.

10. *Personal History* by Katharine Graham. This candid memoir proves that a woman can be rich and thin and still not feel good about herself. Graham grew up with smart, wealthy parents and married a man who was both brilliant and off his rocker. After Phil Graham killed himself, she shed her widow's weeds and a lousy self-image to lead *The Washington Post*. During Watergate, she was warned that her tit would be in the wringer if she exposed bad deeds at the White House. She called the bluff, and the rest is history writ large.

AGES & STAGES

The naturally gorgeous Nicole Kidman dressed herself down, way down, when she played the role of Virginia Woolf in the film version of Michael Cunningham's novel *The Hours*. Her prosthetic nose and tightly wound hair not only recalled Woolf in middle age but also solidified the image of this literary pathbreaker as a homely brainiac.

But don't be so sure that Woolf was a plain Jane. As a girl, she and her sister, Vanessa, were considered quite beautiful. For Woolf, who suffered from depression all her life and ultimately committed suicide, her looks were the least of her problems. Far more relevant to the emotional breakdowns that rolled like waves through her life were the deaths when she was young of three critical figures—her mother, Julia; her half-sister and mother-substitute, Stella; and her father, Leslie.

All this early loss imprinted itself on Woolf's psyche and came through in her writing, with its continual focus on the flow of time. Time is the still water that runs deep and irrevocably through her work. It is an unavoidable element of stream of consciousness, a literary technique Woolf helped develop. Time keeps moving, and that changes everything.

The calendar's relentless progress is one way we measure our lives. Writer Gail Sheehy is known for defining adulthood in terms of decadelong "passages." Many writers divide life into "seasons," starting with the new birth of spring and ending in the soft white cover of winter. Shakespeare famously organized a man's life into seven stages in *As You Like It*.

In the pages ahead, the Babes use five stages to portray the arc of a contemporary woman's life.

1. Coming of Age, Female-Style: In her first twenty or so years, a girl becomes a woman, not only physically but also emotionally. Whether you stay close to home or travel far, your experiences and personality lay the groundwork for what's ahead.

2. Heading Out Into the World: As school days recede, decisions must be made. The good news is that work and/or family are all options. The bad news, as many women have learned, is how hard it is to have a career and raise children at the same time.

3. Settling Down: By your midthirties, you've probably made your bed, either intentionally or otherwise. Still more decisions to be made: Do you want to share it? Will kids be part of the picture?

4. "Enough About Them": By age fifty or so, chances are that your career path is set in pea gravel, if not stone, and/or children are fleeing the nest. You've got crow's feet, but also your second wind.

5. The So-Called Golden Years: A Social Security check is not the only benefit that comes with old age. Experience and wisdom count for something, don't they?

For Virginia Woolf, her own old age became impossible to contemplate. In *To the Lighthouse,* a novel inspired by her mother's early death, she contrasts the lives of two women: the single Lily Briscoe and her older friend, the married Mrs. Ramsay. As the book opens, Mrs. Ramsay is the maternal presence, a figurative lighthouse for her family and their guests during their summer vacations on the Scottish coast. In the last half of the book, which takes place a decade later, her light is gone.

"Mrs. Ramsay! Mrs. Ramsay!" Lily cries out when she returns to the vacation home, trying to summon her dead friend's ghost. The passage of time is painfully apparent, and Lily's future comes into greater focus. To live her own life, or to marry and be subsumed as Mrs. Ramsay's was: Lily's ambivalence is less an indication of Woolf's feminism than her modern sensibility.

In 1980, Carl N. Degler, a history professor at Stanford University, summed up the conflicts that have not gone away in *At Odds: Women and the Family in America from the Revolution to the Present.* Since at least the Reformation, the nuclear family has been the primary experience of most people, he noted. This led to a division of labor that was elevated to tradition under the Victorian notion of separate spheres. Under this system, women were in charge of the home, the children, and the family's moral values.

"And so," Degler says, "the conflict between self and family, which some women in the nineteenth century felt and sometimes fought against, still confronted many married women well into the twentieth century. In fact it remains the central, unresolved tension in the life of a woman in the family."

Of course, decisions about marriage and children affect men's lives, too. But it's rare that they create the same conflict as they do for women who value their independence but also want to have a family. In spite of her depression, Virginia Woolf seems to have had a solid marriage with Leonard, who was her biggest champion and protector of her legacy after she died. But she wrote with some pain about her childlessness—a fact that may surprise those who know her only as the lofty intellectual who articulated a woman's need for "a room of one's own."

Yet deciding whether or not to have children is seldom a casual matter for any woman, and the inability to conceive can be a source of lasting grief. Even in an era when women can have rich lives without raising children, motherhood is not an incidental matter. For most, it's a watershed issue.

The books that lie ahead show women, fictional and real, confronting a wide range of choices through various stages of their lives. Their stories, we hope, will allow you to catch time in a bottle, however briefly, so that you can examine your own options more clearly.

ABOUT COMING OF AGE, FEMALE-STYLE

1. *Hypocrite in a Pouffy White Dress: Tales of Growing Up Groovy and Clueless* by Susan Jane Gilman. This zingy, profane

memoir may not speak for Everywoman but it's so upbeat and full of personality that you'll wish it did. Raised by ex-hippie parents in Manhattan, Gilman carved her own path right up to her wedding day, when she settled for the traditional gown mentioned in her title. Declaring in kindergarten that she would be a ballerina, model, movie star, director, and stewardess, she ended up as none of the above—just a savvy woman who has used humor to smooth out the bumps. Victory!

2. *Once Upon a Quinceañera: Coming of Age in the USA* by Julia Alvarez. This is *Reviving Ophelia* for a new era, told through a look at the Latina version of the coming-out party. The "quince," a celebration marking a girl's fifteenth birthday, attests not only to an increasing Hispanic presence in this country, but also to its pride and economic power. Alvarez, a noted novelist and poet, argues against a tradition that creates "one-night princesses" and for a rite that gives them tools to survive the long haul. "Education is teaching our children to value the right things," she says.

3. *Ghost World* by Daniel Clowes. Move over, Holden Caulfield. This graphic novel's story line captures with perfect pitch the modern version of teenage angst and boredom, following two foul-mouthed childhood friends as they slouch toward adulthood and their paths begin to diverge. Bathed in a pale, ghostly blue, Enid Coleslaw (her name is an anagram of the author's) dreams of disappearing and becoming a "totally different person," while Rebecca Doppelmeyer doesn't want to go anywhere or do anything: "I just want it to be like it was in high school."

4. *How the Light Gets In* by M. J. Hyland. Take teenage angst and add a foreign accent. Voilà: the exchange student from hell. In this sassy novel, sixteen-year-old Lou Cannon trades her poor and dysfunctional family in Australia for a picture-perfect, politically correct household near Chicago. Trouble is, Lou's a compulsive thief and boozer who regards Oreos as a major food group. Gradually, her host parents realize she's more than they bargained for. Hyland captures the vibes of suburban do-gooders and teenage alienation at the same time.

5. *The Secret Life of Bees* by Sue Kidd Monk. Motherless and neglected by her father, a fourteen-year-old white girl named Lily gladly goes on the lam with her black nanny, who's had a run-in with police in the racially polarized South of the early '60s. The duo heads for Tuburon, South Carolina, (the city noted on the back of Lily's mother's picture of a black Virgin Mary). There, they are befriended by three mystical black sisters, August, May, and June, who are beekeepers in this honey of a tale about a teen finding her inner mother and, yes, the life of bees.

6. *When I Was Puerto Rican* by Esmeralda Santiago. When Santiago's father said she would soon be a "teeneyer" and go to America, she didn't believe him. But her mother had had enough of him and Puerto Rico. In this lively memoir, Santiago describes her transition from a *jibara* (a rural Puerto Rican) "who longed for the green quiet of a tropical afternoon" to "a hybrid who would never forgive the uprooting." From the Brooklyn projects to Harvard, she didn't stop to think about how far she'd come: "It might jinx the momentum."

7. *Without a Map* by Meredith Hall. It didn't matter that she was a straight-A student. When Hall became pregnant at age sixteen in the mid-1960s, her parents made clear that this wiped out the value of everything else she had done. At age eighteen she sums up how she no longer relates to her peers: "I have a baby floating somewhere in the world. I am an old woman." Isolated but hardly alone (see *The Girls Who Went Away* in 10 for Adapting and Adopting), Hall reconciles the dark days with the time years later when she meets her grown child. "Whatever else may have gone wrong, whatever of grief and loss is carried by each of us, so too is love."

8. *I Am Charlotte Simmons* by Tom Wolfe. In this doorstop of a novel, the scenes of excessive drunkenness and mindless hooking up at the fictional Dupont University may be exaggerated (although Wolfe, a former journalist, heavily researches his fiction). But the class differences he underscores are not. Charlotte Simmons, a poor, naïve girl from the North Carolina mountains who "aspires to the life of the mind," desperately needs to feel special "no matter how she achieved it." The elite classmates who corrupt her already know they are special. They can afford to waste their time in school.

9. *The Golden Road: Notes on My Gentrification* by Caille Millner. From drug dealers in the 'hood to limousine liberals at Harvard, Millner covered a broader than usual range of values and personality types during her teen years. Looking back, she feels like members of both groups were so concerned with fitting the mold that they sacrificed their individual identity. If you hang

IN PRAISE OF MARGARET ATWOOD

In the 1970s, women were busting through ceilings, glass and otherwise, and there was a hard edge to the feminism that captured the headlines. Women's rights couldn't be taken for granted, because there seemed so few. A relative handful of women were prominent in politics, the professions, or the boardroom. I came out of college feeling like the smallest carrot in the patch, and I was: My first postcollege job in a newsroom was as a copy aide, running errands and sorting mail.

Margaret Atwood came to my rescue. The Canadian writer was writing novels that articulated all the doubts and conflicts I was feeling. In *The Edible Woman* (1969), *Surfacing* (1972), *Lady Oracle* (1976), and *Life Before Man* (1979), she delved into the contemporary female psyche and explained me to myself.

In her later novel, *The Handmaid's Tale* (1986), Atwood came at sexism with a slap, depicting a future world in which environmental degradation has diminished the fertility rate, and in the name of survival, women's lives are tightly controlled. But I prefer the more textured and personal approach in her earlier fiction. For instance, the central figure in *The Edible Woman* is unable to eat and gradually realizes the reason is that she's being swallowed up by her prospective marriage. In *Surfacing*, a young woman who goes searching for her father in the Quebec woods discovers another mission: to come to terms with herself and her recent abortion.

In these earlier works, it's less woman against man and more woman and man caught in the vortex of a confusing world. It's about realizing something's not right and struggling to define why. Rereading them reminds me why Atwood is one of the finest writers around. Given the range of fiction and poetry she has produced in the past four decades, the Babes couldn't decide which deserved to be singled out. So this is our way of recommending Atwood's work: by the bunch.

~ Ellen

too closely with any particular subculture, you put yourself at risk, she says. Millner has no problem with trying on different personas. "The trouble arises when we start believing in our creations and put them up for sale."

10. *Things I Want My Daughters to Know: A Small Book About the Big Issues in Life* by Alexandra Stoddard. This compendium of motherly advice from a pro on personal fulfillment preaches self-reliance, gratitude, and perseverance with style. "To be human is to experience pain and overcome it," she writes, and her upbeat attitude makes playing through the pain seem not only possible, but life affirming. Noting that familiarity breeds contempt, she devises a "five-hour rule" for fraternizing. Another tidbit: "When you discover something you love, stock up."

ABOUT HEADING OUT INTO THE WORLD

1. *The Wonder Spot* by Melissa Bank. "I never expected anyone in my family to change, and especially not my father, who changed first and most profoundly: He died," says Sophie Applebaum, the wisecracking narrator of this novel about the vicissitudes of family ties. Sophie, who grew up in a Jewish family in suburban Pennsylvania, breaks away to live in Manhattan. There, she teaches herself to type, juggles a parade of boyfriends, and negotiates her ever-evolving relationships with a mother who has moved on, two very different brothers, and an insufferable grandmother. No wonder she feels like "a solid trying to do a liquid's job."

2. *The Emperor's Children* by Claire Messud. After wavering between "Big Ideas and a party," Marina Thwaite and two college friends at thirty finally are staggering into the "Realm of Adult Sobriety" via a mismatched marriage and disastrous affairs. Set on the eve of 9/11, this smart comedy of manners takes perfect aim at the self-satisfied intellectual elite (represented by Marina's father, the "emperor" of the title) that so ill-prepared these overgrown children for the terrorism of the real world: "The revolution belonged to other people now, far away from them, and it was real."

3. *The Curse of the Singles Table: A True Story of 1001 Nights Without Sex* by Suzanne Schlosberg. When speed dating, Match.com, exotic trips, volunteering, and feng shui don't produce Mr. Right (or even Mr. Remote Possibility), Schlosberg marks her streak—more than 1001 days without sex—by completing an Alaskan bike trek known as the Arctic Ocean Ride of Pain. No, this isn't the plot of a wacky chick-lit novel; it's the life story of a very funny writer. The self-described "Cal Ripken of celibacy," Schlosberg finally ends her streak by just letting go. "Maybe all you can do is be ready."

4. *Straight Up and Dirty: A Memoir* by Stephanie Klein. At twenty-nine, Klein's two-and-a-half-year-old "starter marriage" comes to an end. This is the raunchy tale of Klein's recovery, which includes hot sex with new men but, more important, Klein's honesty about her marriage. His infidelity fueled the collapse, she notes, but so did her superficial idea of what constitutes wedded bliss. "It wasn't about the charming Jewish doctor with the Ivy League education and George Clooney looks. That's what you look for when you're incomplete."

5. *Undue Influence* by Anita Brookner. Aloneness seems the natural state for Brookner's heroines, who all fit under the category Women Who Think Too Much. Given their tendency to brood, it's little surprise that the star of this novel, Claire Pitt, fears the single life. Consciously or not, at age twenty-nine she schemes to follow her mother's pattern and marry an older man. But watch out for best-laid plans—especially when you fail to tell the other party what you intend to do. Either way, this is a sharp-eyed look at the urge to tie the knot for social and financial stability.

6. *Necessary Sins: A Memoir* by Lynn Darling. "All marriages begin in a myth, a carapace under which the real marriage takes shape," Darling writes. In her case, the myth contained her young free-spirited self and an older husband who left his first marriage and three children so that the two of them could wed. Her memoir is built around the idea that he gave up so much, while she was the one who needed to grow up and become a wife, stepmother, mother—and, in startlingly short order, a widow. Darling's memoir captures the way love stays afloat on a sea of conflicting emotions and events.

7. *Maybe Baby: 28 Writers Tell the Truth About Skepticism, Infertility, Baby Lust, Childlessness, Ambivalence and How They Made the Biggest Decision of Their Lives* edited by Lori Leibovich. Based on Salon's series, To Breed or Not to Breed, this absorbing anthology (which Leibovich edited when she was pregnant) covers a whole gamut of choices, from "no, thanks, not for me" and "on the fence" to "taking the leap." For the first time in history, parenthood is a choice. Even men face the "daddy dilemma," Leibovich says. "All of the old rules about childbearing no longer apply."

8. *Waiting for Daisy: A Tale of Two Continents, Three Religions, Five Infertility Doctors, an Oscar, an Atomic Bomb, a Romantic Night, and One Woman's Quest to Become a Mother* by Peggy Orenstein. A writer known for promoting women's independence admits the irony in her long and obsessive journey to have a child. At first reluctant, Orenstein changes her mind with a vengeance and nearly destroys her marriage when she fails. "It feels so unfair," she tells her husband. "It's not unfair. Unfair is when my friend Lynn died at forty-two," he snaps back. The title tips you off to a happy ending, but getting there is the trick.

9. *Baby Proof: A Novel* by Emily Griffin. Deceptively breezy, with a delicious O. Henry ending, Griffin's novel is about babies—not having them, that is. "I never wanted to be a mother," narrator

Claudia admits. Her husband, Ben, didn't want children, either—until he did. When his change of heart precipitates a divorce, Claudia suddenly can't shake the baby issue. Surrounded by family and friends grappling with infertility, a miscarriage, adoption, and the not-so-simple act of raising children, she has to ponder her own question about procreation: What is she willing to do for love?

10. *A Life's Work: On Becoming a Mother* by Rachel Cusk. British novelist Cusk confronts new motherhood with the tool she knows best, a pen, and the results are delightfully acerbic and far above average. Allusions to the likes of Edith Wharton, Coleridge, and *The Secret Garden* embroider her larger theme, which is the strange beauty and terror of being subsumed by another human being. Looking forward, "I see my daughter hurrying away from me, hurtling towards her future, and in that sight I recognize my ending, my frontier, the boundary of my life."

ABOUT SETTLING DOWN

1. *Mating in Captivity: Unlocking Erotic Intelligence* by Esther Perel. Don't just blame the kids, work, or antidepressants for the lack of sex in your marriage. Combining closeness and desire is never easy, warns New York therapist Perel in this unorthodox look at an age-old problem. Eroticism requires separateness, the antithesis of intimacy. So are sexless marriages inevitable? No, she says, but old lovers need to re-create the natural distance they enjoyed as new lovers. It takes work. "Nurturing eroticism in the home is an act of open defiance."

2. *Lies at the Altar: The Truth About Great Marriages* by Dr. Robin L. Smith. So here's a shocker from a celebrity psychologist: Honesty is the basis for a good marriage. True, the insights in this how-to won't surprise you, but they are a good guide for making the most of your bedrock relationship. Some key points: Marriage is meant for grown-ups. Sexual fidelity matters, but so, too, does emotional availability. Can you name five positive qualities you each bring to your union? If the negatives are on the tip of your tongue, it's time to consider a tune-up.

3. *Le Mariage* by Diane Johnson. The rich and famous don't settle down quite like the rest of us—especially if you are an Oregonian transplant living in a chateau outside of Paris next door to a tempting aristocrat. In this astute comedy of manners Johnson returns to the field she mined in *Le Divorce*, roasting the self-absorbed lives of American expats and their French hosts. A murder, a stolen manuscript, a feud over hunting rights provide the backdrop to her astute observations about marriage and love, international style. The cultural clashes are real—and hilarious.

4. *I Don't Know How She Does It: The Life of Katy Reddy, Working Mother* by Allison Pearson. Katy Reddy can make a mince pie for a child's school party, soothe her increasingly overshadowed husband's ego, flirt with the idea of an affair, mourn her friend's death, and juggle nine different currencies in five different time zones—all before breakfast. How does she do it? Pearson's comic novel, the working mom's version of *Bridget Jones's Diary*, also told in diary form with the same understated British humor, hints at the answer: day by hectic day.

5. *Life Among the Savages* by Shirley Jackson. Jackson, author of the scary short story "The Lottery," took a break from her dark side to write this classic about raising her brood in the 'burbs. First published in 1948, it now has the patina of a classic, wrapping humor and nostalgia in an Erma Bombeck–like trek through Jackson's household. Beneath the wit lies the bittersweet truth about motherhood: "One of the most unnerving, and least original, observations I have made about my children," she writes, is that "they tend to grow older."

6. *After This* by Alice McDermott. Shift down a few decades to the family of John and Mary Keane, an Irish Catholic couple living through the turbulent '60s in this novel about how one family confronts the winds of social change. The answer: with difficulty. At one point Mary slaps her unwed pregnant daughter and asks rhetorically, "How much more can I take?" The answer goes without saying. For couples like the Keanes, the center will hold, but it ends up looking quite different than either of them anticipated.

7. *Operating Instructions: A Journal of My Son's First Year* by Anne Lamott. At thirty-five, Lamott wings her way into single motherhood via an unexpected pregnancy. This diary of her adventure captures the usual feelings that go with giving birth—joy, worry, exhaustion—but with the candor that makes Lamott's story stand out. The miracle of Sam's birth and his "Yoda smile" are juxtaposed against her fight to have the father acknowledge him and the sorrow of losing her best friend to breast cancer. Of new motherhood, she concludes, "I think we're all pretty crazy on this bus."

8. *MotherKind* by Jayne Anne Phillips. The circle of life comes into sharp focus in this tender novel about a thirtysomething whose first pregnancy coincides with her mother's slow death from cancer. The all-consuming nature of new motherhood ("Most women thought they were looking for men, not babies. Kate thought now that they were wrong. . . .") contrasts with her own mother's quiet attentiveness to her daughter's new responsibilities. The myriad complications of modern family life come together in a story that, like the ties that bind, has "a starry radiance too bright to observe."

9. *Mommy Wars: Stay-at-Home and Career Moms Face Off on Their Choices, Their Lives, Their Families* by Leslie Morgan Steiner. Stay-at-home mothers and career moms duking it out? Judging from these essays, the real conflict lies within each mom's heart. Actress Monica Buckley Price stays at home with her autistic son. CEO Ann Misiaszek Sarnoff combines motherhood and ambition. "There are no easy answers," says editor Steiner, a part-time working mother. "Just ask yourself, would you want to be your kid?" suggests columnist Carolyn Hax. "Then make peace with your choices from there."

10. *Strike Sparks: Selected Poems, 1980–2002* by Sharon Olds. Olds's poetry is filled with images of family life—her son's first bath (soaped up "like an armful of buttered noodles"), children sleeping (her daughter "in abandon and sealed completion," her son, "one knee up as if he is climbing sharp stairs"), but she's no sentimentalist. In her hands, the details of a woman's everyday life reveal something strikingly profound—like those seven-year-olds at her son's birthday party: "short men, men in first grade . . . jostling, jockeying for place . . . a room of small bankers."

THAT SAY, "ENOUGH ABOUT THEM"

1. *Prime: Adventures and Advice on Sex, Love and the Sensual Years* by Dr. Pepper Schwartz. Schwartz, a sociologist known for her sex research, lays herself bare as she describes her life after the end of a twenty-three-year marriage. Imbued with a strong sex drive and "buckets of research" confirming the value of body contact, she cultivates relationships for the sex of it and lets the chips fall (not always softly). She notes the risk of STDs and emotional damage but says that, with a "capacity to love that is unequaled," women in their fifties should follow her lead and go boldly into the dating world.

2. *Naked on the Page: The Misadventures of My Unmarried Midlife* by Jane Ganahl. One year shy of fifty, Ganahl was a

IN PRAISE OF LATE BLOOMERS

In our last year of high school, a friend and I started a list of people who had achieved success late in life. Every year we added more names to our roster of late bloomers, sensing perhaps that we, too, would be needing some time to blossom. As we grew older, the age line pushed ever upward. When both of us became journalists, our list came to include more and more writers. I was especially interested in the women authors who took their time to make their mark. Here are my favorites and their accomplishments. I hope they inspire you to compile your own list, tailoring it to your own dreams of success:

Sharon Olds, American poet, at 38: first volume of poetry, *Satan Says*.

Betty Friedan, American feminist, at 42: *The Feminine Mystique*; at 72, *The Fountain of Age*.

Kate Chopin, American author, at 47: first novel, *At Fault*; at 49, the classic, *The Awakening*.

Emily Post, style maven, at 49: best-selling book of manners, *Etiquette in Society, in Business, in Politics, and at Home*.

Julia Child, chef (See "Babes We Love"), at 49: first cookbook, *Mastering the Art of French Cooking*; at 51, started her popular TV show, *The French Chef*.

Gertrude Jekyll, English gardener, at 53: *A Gardener's Testament*.

Mary Midgley, English philosopher, at 56: *Beast and Man: The Roots of Human Nature*.

Mary O'Hara, American screenwriter and novelist, at 56: *My Friend Flicka*.

Anna Sewell, English novelist, at 57: *Black Beauty*.

Penelope Fitzgerald, English writer, at 58: a biography of pre-Raphaelite artist Edward Burne-Jones; at 62, won Booker Prize for her novel *Offshore.*

Laura Ingalls Wilder, American writer, at 65: first volume of the *Little House on the Prairie* series.

Mary Wesley, British children's book writer, at 57: two children's books, *Speaking Terms* and *The Sixth Seal*; at 70, her first novel, *Jumping the Queue.*

Harriet Doerr, American writer, at 74: first novel, *Stones for Ibarra.*

Agatha Christie, British mystery author and playwright, at 62: *The Mousetrap*, the longest-running play in the world.

Helen Hooven Santmyer, American author, at 88: best-selling novel, *And Ladies of the Club.*

~ Margo

"single woman cliché"—divorced with a grown daughter and three cats—when she launched her column on middle-aged dating for the San Francisco *Chronicle.* She uses her forum to describe a whole series of romantic dead-ends and deadbeats with self-deprecating humor. Ganahl isn't an advice maven, but she's clearly up on love. Just don't count on it. Instead, "find your inner busy body and get her involved in as many people's lives as possible."

3. *The Summer Before the Dark* by Doris Lessing. Feminists celebrate Lessing's ample novel *The Golden Notebook* but this shorter work of fiction by the Nobel Prize winner also reveals her view of the female condition. After decades as an accommodating wife and mother, an attractive English homemaker spends a summer abroad going through detox, metaphorically speaking. She analyzes a life of striving for male attention, "twitching like a puppet to those strings." This is less a radical manifesto than an honest appraisal of how a woman's sexual power changes focus as she ages.

4. *I Feel Bad About My Neck: And Other Thoughts on Being a Woman* by Nora Ephron. "Our faces are lies and our necks are the truth. You have to cut down a redwood tree to see how old it is, but you wouldn't have to, if it had a neck," says comic writer Ephron in this book of essays on middle-age woes. Recalling Gertrude Stein's famous deathbed inquiry, "What's the answer?" Ephron asks her own, more pressing, questions about life: "Are we really going to have to spend our last years avoiding bread, especially now that bread in America is so unbelievably delicious? And what about chocolate? There's a question for you, Gertrude Stein—what about chocolate?"

5. *Fear of Fifty: A Midlife Memoir* by Erica Jong. Raised as a good girl in the '50s, Jong takes stock as she reaches her fifties in this exuberant memoir. She comes clean about her writing career, multiple divorces and affairs, parenting ("Surrendering to motherhood means surrendering to interruption"), current midlife marriage (ironically, for the author of *Fear of Flying*, to an amateur pilot), and lingering fear of becoming her mother. What's a member of the "whiplash generation," caught between a stay-at-

home mom and an empowered daughter, to do? Embrace the fierce and the tender.

6. *Going Gray: What I Learned About Beauty, Sex, Work, Motherhood, Authenticity and Everything Else That Really Matters* by Anne Kreamer. At forty-nine, after twenty-five years of hair coloring, Kreamer traded in her brown helmet for natural gray. Here, the former Nickelodeon exec and mother of two girls surveys the pros and cons of that decision, so often resisted by youth-obsessed baby boomers. One surprise? Men prefer the natural look—especially in Europe, where "tan tights and bad shoes and gaudy make-up are much more likely to be a strike against you than gray hair."

7. *Tales of Graceful Aging From the Planet of Denial* by Nicole Hollander. The spirit of Sylvia, Hollander's sardonic comic strip character, pervades this tongue-in-cheek "memoir" (along with her cats). Constantly summoning three girlfriends to her side for moral support (it's more like six or seven in real life, she later admits), Hollander ponders the choices of aging: Disgusting Herbal Remedies or Something Delightful, with Vodka. Plastic Surgery or a Really Good Haircut. "Okay, sixty is the new forty. Now it's mandatory to become a second-wind achiever. Just what I needed, more stress, more pressure."

8. *Without Reservations: The Travels of an Independent Woman* by Alice Steinbach. After years of writing newspaper profiles, Steinbach wanted to experience life, not just observe it, she admits

in this charming chronicle of her "Year of Living Dangerously."
No, she didn't scale mountains. She went solo to Europe. Walking "in the foothills of adventure" was gutsy enough for this divorced mother of two grown sons: romance in Paris, ballroom
dancing in Oxford, almost getting mugged in Rome. On her last
day: "This is what I will have forever. The memory of this moment, of rain falling on Venice."

9. *How to Be a Middle-Aged Babe* by Marilyn Suzanne Miller. If
people are starting to call you "ma'am," this hilarious oversize book
full of scenes reminiscent of *Saturday Night Live* sketches is here to
help. Miller, a former *SNL* writer, covers such useful topics as Lipo-
suction You Can Do at Home, a Worldwide Map of Ladies' Rooms,
Cardiac Pulmonary Resuscitation during a Blow Job, and a Babe
Fun-Reading List (she recommends *Oedipus* and *Cherry Ames, Student Nurse*). "Grow old (or middle) exuberantly," Miller urges,
adding sardonically, "As my mother would say, 'What else?'"

10. *At Blackwater Pond: Mary Oliver Reads Mary Oliver.* In
menopause, the maternal urge moves toward nature and animals.
No wonder Oliver's poems are so popular with baby boomers. For
nearly thirty years, she has been the poet of the natural world,
rarely writing a poem that doesn't begin or end outdoors. In her
seventies, she produced this combo book and CD, reading forty-
two poems from various collections. Like her memorable sip of
water from Blackwater Pond, these verses are guaranteed to wake
your bones: "I hear them / deep inside me, whispering / oh what
is that beautiful thing / that just happened?"

ABOUT THE SO-CALLED GOLDEN YEARS

1. *The Art of Aging: A Doctor's Prescription for Well-Being* by Sherwin B. Nuland. Sure, aging brings woes, but it can also bring wisdom. The wise stay connected to others, maintain their bodies, and tap into their creativity, says Nuland, the author of *How We Die*. Just look at the active lives chronicled here: Dr. Michael Debakey, who kept up a peripatetic pace into his nineties; Patricia Neal, whose stroke didn't stop her acting career; and Mariam Gabler, a widow who turned to writing after her husband died. Who needs a fountain of youth?

2. *A Round-Heeled Woman: My Late-Life Adventures in Sex and Romance* by Jane Juska. After enduring a shotgun wedding, single parenting, obesity, and analysis, Juska ran a personal ad in *The New York Review of Books*: "Before I turn 67, I would like to have sex with a man I like. If you want to talk first, Trollope works for me." In this disarming memoir, she reveals the touching (in both senses) encounters she had, thanks to Trollope: "Life just keeps coming at you. But every so often, you can catch a piece of it and make it do what you want it to."

3. *Evening* by Susan Minot. Ann Lord is dying. Wrapped in the cocoon of pain medication as friends and family stand by, the sixty-five-year-old escapes the present for the past. In a novel about one life lived bravely and passionately, it's clear Ann was a woman who liked men, and they returned the compliment. Yet "branded into her forehead with a hot iron" is a brief affair forty years before that she remembers with more clarity than her two marriages. "Hope is a terrible thing," she muses. "People could always change and always hurt you."

4. *The Fountain of Age* by Betty Friedan. Our society usually blanks out images of the elderly, but this impressively researched exposé places "vitally aging people" front and center. The author of *The Feminine Mystique*, who died in 2006, wanted to bust what she called "the age mystique," the idea that old age is an unhappy time. With seniors living healthier and more active lives than ever before, what matters, says Friedan, is for seniors to make their own decisions: "free and joyous, living with pain, saying what we really think and feel at last."

5. *The Riddle of Life and Death: "Tell Me a Riddle,"* by Tillie Olsen and *"The Death of Ivan Ilych,"* by Leo Tolstoy. Part of a thought-provoking series dubbed Two by Two, where works on similar subjects by a man and woman are united, this book includes Olsen's story about Eva, a Jewish mother in twentieth-century America, and Tolstoy's tale of Ivan, a smug aristocrat in czarist Russia. Both are dying and, though in tremendous pain, reflecting on their lives. Eva, worn out from living for others, can give no more. Ivan, who placed creature comforts over family, realizes too late he had not given enough. Both are a reminder, says Jules Chametzky in the intro, "to live life better."

6. *Rules for Old Men Waiting* by Peter Pouncey. Historian Robert MacIver has lost his wife, Margaret, his soul mate and the one who stood between him and the "blood-and-guts, slash-and-burn pillage party" of his career in academia. In this novel, the "fierce old Scot" soldiers on alone in his isolated home on Cape Cod, displacing his grief by writing a story of courage and companionship that's set among Flanders fields and the trench warfare of World War I. In a final act of defiance against death, he holds on to his independence, engages the imagination, and remembers a cherished woman.

7. *No! I Don't Want to Join a Book Club* by Virginia Ironside. Don't tell Marie Sharp old age is a time to whoop it up. The sassy, smart, and postmenopausal heroine of this coming-to-old-age novel doesn't want to be bungee jumping at seventy or trekking across country at eighty. She wants to be left alone with her bunions and watery eyes. Well, not completely alone. She has to look after a new grandson, a dying gay friend, and a girlfriend who's been dumped by a younger guy. Who has time to join a book club?

8. *Julie & Romeo* by Jeanne Ray. What would you do if your widowed mother or father began dating? The children of Julie and Romeo are hardly thrilled with that prospect in this light-hearted novel about steamy late-in-life romance. To complicate matters—and with an obvious nod to Shakespeare's famous pairing—Ray provides an added twist: the trysting widow and widower hail from two bitterly feuding families who own the town's rival florist shops. Happily, Ray doesn't stick with the bard's doomed ending. Age does have its privileges.

9. *Granny D.: Walking Across America in My 90th Year* by Doris Haddock with Dennis Burke. You don't have to be interested in campaign-finance reform, the reason for Haddock's protest walk, to enjoy spending time with this feisty nonagenarian who refuses to think old. Beginning in California, she crosses the Mohave Desert on foot, stops at a strip club, and celebrates two birthdays (including her ninetieth) before arriving in Washington, D.C., fourteen months later. "I apologize for preaching far more than I intended," she concludes, "but I'm sure you skipped through the worst of it."

10. *Can't Wait to Get to Heaven* by Fannie Flagg. It's curtains for eighty-nine-year-old Elner Shimfissle after she falls out of a tree while picking figs. Or is it? Pronounced dead, she meets her deceased sister, Thomas Edison, and—glory be—her Maker, before medical intervention snatches her from the long arm of the Rest Assured Funeral Home. Back on planet Earth, she has some crazy wisdom for her niece, the doctor, and a lawyer circling her potential malpractice case. Flagg delivers theology with a side of laughter and a recipe for the caramel cake that Elner almost tasted during her trip to the other side.

THE BABE INSIDE

Joan Didion is at war with herself. A masterful writer who has used fiction and essays to spell out the anxieties of our age, she suffers from migraine headaches that seem to be her body's manifestation of her worry about the world.

These stealth bombers come with predictable reliability, crippling her for days at a time. Yet she has learned not to fight them.

"At first every apprehension is magnified, every anxiety a pounding terror," she writes in an essay aptly titled "In Bed." "Then the pain comes, and I concentrate only on that. Right there is the usefulness of migraine, there in that self-imposed yoga, the concentration on the pain."

Analyzing her headaches with the same cool detachment with which she takes the pulse of society and politics, Didion realizes that she's a product of her own introspection. She accepts her migraines as the negative manifestation of the intensity that fuels her art. It's hard to look at yourself with the distance that brings such clarity. But don't you sometimes wish you could?

In this section, the Babes take the measure of the inner woman. Here's where we address how you feel about yourself and how that attitude is influenced by other factors—society's expectations, friends, family. Here's where we offer ideas for taking control of your inner voice through spiritual and artistic growth.

Any consideration of a woman's emotional and physical health can't ignore appearance, and that merits two separate lists—one that weighs attractiveness in terms of your features, the other by the pound. In the past few decades, the definition of beauty has grown to multicultural dimensions. But even while studies show Americans getting heavier, the feminine ideal remains model-worthy and stick straight. Judging from the celebrities whose svelte bodies serve as our models, the message is clear: Fat is not where it's at. This makes weight not just a health issue. It's also a head issue.

So what's a Babe to do? Well, for starters, avoid taking cues from TV, advertising, and our impersonal, media-mad culture. Don't let those guys do all the talking. Your inner voice deserves to be heard.

In search of our own voices, the Babes are guided by the three Rs—reading, 'riting, reflecting. Use good books like the ones we suggest to feed your thoughts. Combine them with keeping a journal, if that helps. (You can always gift wrap it for your therapist.)

Thanks to science, we now know that depression has to do with serotonin levels, and soon the human genome will be mapped to the last eyelash. But health is more than the sum of these parts. In his collaboration with Buddhist monks, psychologist Daniel Goleman has calculated the flow of emotions through their brains to show how their disciplined meditation makes an imprint. Other research points to a similar conclusion: The mind can be trained. You *do* have some control over your thoughts and feelings.

Your body can play tricks on you, as does Didion's. But a dent is being made in the biology-is-destiny argument that has been stirring in the bushes since Darwin.

Calibrating your inner voice starts with the stories you tell yourself. Mere facts will not suffice. The brain works best with narrative construction, says Steven Pinker, a psychology professor at the Massachusetts Institute of Technology. "Human behavior makes the most sense when it is explained in terms of beliefs and desires, not in terms of volts and grams," he writes in *How the Mind Works*. In other words, formulas are swell for robots, but we're hardwired to learn and explain ourselves through storytelling.

Psychologists say it's not only the stories you tell, but also how you tell them, that determine how you live your life. In *The Redemptive Self: Stories Americans Live By,* Northwestern University professor Dan P. McAdams lays out his research on the importance of how experiences are framed.

For some people, that frame is pretty dark. Even supposedly happy events, like a wedding, are recalled less for the celebration than for the guest who drank too much or the relative who made an insulting remark. In contrast, the individuals McAdams calls "generative adults" rework even negative events to show how long-term gain trumped short-term pain. It's not as if getting kicked out of school or going through a divorce was pleasant, they say. But because it led to a positive experience—a new and more beneficial learning opportunity, or a more suitable partner—it is viewed in a beneficial light.

In literary terms, the generative adult is the redemptive self, a staple of storytelling. Here's the pattern: First comes early luck or blessings, at least as compared to less fortunate peers. Second is the idea of being chosen—for a special or separate destiny. Third comes the belief that, even when surrounded by evil, positive values such as honesty and devotion remain intact.

The variations on this theme are endless, but the narrative arc remains constant. Through the stories we tell ourselves and those told to us, we open up the possibility for self-discovery and rejuvenation.

ON THE LUST FOR BEAUTY

1. *The Naked Woman: A Study of the Female Body* by Desmond Morris. As a zoologist, Morris sees every female as beautiful, "the brilliant end-point of millions of years of evolution." But each woman enhances nature's gifts in her own way, says the author of *The Naked Ape* in this hair-to-feet tour. What is considered beautiful depends on where—and when—you live. Take teeth. Modern society prefers them gleaming white. But in Elizabeth I's time, they were blackened to show that women were rich enough for their teeth to rot. Hey, sugar was expensive.

2. *Survival of the Prettiest: The Science of Beauty* by Nancy Etcoff. Humans are hardwired to care about appearance, psychologist Etcoff claims—a fixation tied to reproduction and survival of the species. Yes, she allows, "lookism" ranks right up there with sexism and racism, and is "howlingly unfair." So: Deal with it. Etcoff tackles every aspect—height, weight, penis size (we're not kidding)—to argue that our tastes are evolutionary, not arbitrary. Given this argument, would it surprise you to learn that American women spend more on making themselves pretty than improving their minds?

3. *The Beauty Myth* by Naomi Wolf. Wait a minute, says Wolf, refuting the biological determinism argument of authors such as Etcoff. In this book, first published in 1991, she makes the case that even brainiacs and achievers get docked if they lack the "Professional Beauty Qualification"—that is, they don't look like the women who play them in movies. Wolf's nurture-over-nature argument blames men and the political institutions they created. She agrees with Ectoff and Morris that women care deeply about how they look. But the three could have one heck of a debate about why.

4. *Fairest* by Gail Carson Levine. In this young-adult novel, Levine cleverly plays on the double meaning of "the fairest of them all." Challenging the impossible beauty standards classic fairy tales have imposed on women, her heroine is a gawky girl with pulpy cheeks. Of course, Ava eventually lands the prince (who cares if his ears stick out?), but always fair-minded, she never blames others (even the pretty ones) for her low self-esteem. She knows she has been her own worst critic: "I'd avoided looking in actual mirrors, but I'd gazed constantly in the mirror of my mind and always hated what I showed myself."

5. *Beauty Junkies: Inside Our $15 Billion Obsession with Cosmetic Surgery* by Alex Kuczynski. Ready for a lift or tuck? You may take a pass after reading this exposé about extreme makeovers. Whether talking about Botox or going under the knife, journalist Kuczynski uses worst-case scenarios to question surgical alterations and the industry that promotes them. Her advice: Focus on building character, not a "beautiful carapace." She's a reformed sinner: Happy with an eye lift, she followed up with an injection that gave her a fat lip, much worry—and a change of heart.

6. *The Bluest Eye* by Toni Morrison. In this 1965 novel, Morrison explores the impact racial rejection has had on the self-image of black girls. The story is set in the 1940s, when affirmations such as "Black is beautiful" were still decades away, when "all the world had agreed that a blue-eyed, yellow-haired, pink-skinned doll was what every girl child treasured." No wonder Pecola Breedlove, a little black girl living in a troubled household, yearns for the blue eyes of a little white girl: "*If* those eyes of hers were different, that is to say, beautiful, she herself would be different."

7. *Stacked: A 32DDD Reports from the Front* by Susan Seligson. Each year 300,000 U.S. women get breast implants; 150,000 go in for breast reductions. In this informative and funny tour of "Titsburg," Seligson investigates the not-only-male obsession with boobs (the term women prefer; men use more colorful euphemisms). She pursues exotic dancer Maxi Mounds and reports on the topfreedom movement (Slogan: Nipples Not Napalm).

With breasts the size of "the USS *Nimitz* anchored in a pond," she is refreshingly nonjudgmental, even forgiving that driver who yelled "nice tits" and then cursed her when he ended up plowing into a lamppost.

8. *My Mother's Wedding Dress: The Life & Afterlife of Clothes* by Justine Picardie. The quest for beauty usually involves the perfect outfit. In this look at how clothes shape you, an editor of British *Vogue* scours the pages of literature, the halls of haute couture, and her own closet (alas, her mother's wedding dress, a black cocktail sheath, is only a memory). On her list of best-dressed heroines: Pippi Longstocking (mismatched stockings and all), Miss Havisham in *Great Expectations* (for inspiring vintage chic), and the title character with her silver dress in Daphne du Maurier's *Rebecca*.

9. *The Collection: A Novel* by Gioia Diliberto. A haze of cigarettes, mounds of gleaming fabric, and the click and slice of scissors permeate Diliberto's novel about the fashion revolution in post–World War II Paris. The battle among rival designers is seen through the eyes of a young seamstress. But the star is the demanding and eccentric Chanel, who converted the black mourning of war into the little black dress of chic. Why should you care? If it weren't for Coco, you might still be wearing ruffled crinolines.

10. *Kabul Beauty School: An American Woman Goes Behind the Veil* by Deborah Rodriguez. When hairdresser Rodriguez volunteered to go to Afghanistan after 9/11, she was hardly the typical do-gooder: "Crazy Deb" sported spiked red hair, gobs o' makeup, and the moxie to start a beauty school. Her move is both liberating and incendiary: False eyelashes and hair extensions are a source of profit but also suspicion where women are chattel. Forced to leave the country for her safety, Rodriguez says of her Afghani sisters, "I sometimes wonder if I've done as much for them as they've done for me."

THAT TIP THE SCALES

1. *Rethinking Thin: The New Science of Weight Loss—and the Myths and Realities of Dieting* by Gina Kolata. Framing her book around a study that compared low-calorie to low-carb, Kolata sides with neither diet. Instead, the *New York Times* reporter complains that a scant 4 percent of women have the 110-pound profile of Jennifer Aniston, so it's time to readjust our thinking, if not the charts. Claiming that America's obesity epidemic is overstated, she gives comfort to the well-padded, but leaves you wondering where plump leaves off and real problems start.

2. *Fast Food Nation* by Eric Schlosser. Schlosser has no doubt that the obesity epidemic is real. He targets McDonald's and its kin for putting on the pounds. Fast food and the meat-packing industry get the one-two punch as Schlosser takes you on a tour of ranches, slaughterhouses, and the Ray A. Kroc Museum. The victims, he says, are not only the consumers of calorie-packed Happy Meals, but also those working in unsafe conditions to produce them. If he's right that "a nation's diet can be more revealing than its art or literature," America is deep-fried in more ways than one.

3. *French Women Don't Get Fat* by Mireille Guiliano. A promenade. A romantic interlude. A good hearty laugh. These are Guiliano's secrets for staying thin and for being happy. She rejects the American notion of "no pain, no gain." If you adopt even a fraction of the French attitude toward food and life, she says, "managing weight would cease to be a terror, an obsession, and reveal its true nature as part of the art of living." If you walk enough, love enough, and laugh enough, you won't have to be afraid of crème fraîche.

4. *Food and Loathing: A Life Measured Out in Calories* by Betsy Lerner. Lerner has been a plus-size gal all her life, a compulsive overeater who also had depression and manic-depressive disorder on her plate. A tough order, but reading her story, you'll marvel at her resilience. A career woman, wife, and mother, she used her smarts and humor to transcend her weight struggle and the terrible body image that's reflected in this diary entry: *"Wore shorts to therapy!* Truly a victory for a girl who believed her thighs were grounds for execution."

5. *Good in Bed* by Jennifer Weiner. In Weiner's first novel, twenty-eight-year-old Candace Shapiro is the poster child of excess adipose. With a former boyfriend advertising their romance as his outreach to the overweight, she feels like "Ally McBeal and Bridget Jones put together, which was probably about how much I

weighed." But the sum of her pounds soon becomes the least of Candace's problems in this story of love and loss and love again. Poignant and funny, this book rises above its chick-lit label and puts weight in the proper perspective.

6. *The Weight of It* by Amy Wilensky. Amy admits this story of weight is not completely hers to tell. It was her sister, Alison, whose binge eating led to morbid obesity. It was Alison who was "ignored, made fun of, scoffed at, disparaged." And it was Alison, at risk for diabetes, high blood pressure, stroke, heart attack, and almost every type of cancer, who later opted for gastric bypass surgery. But Amy's memoir underscores an overlooked but often experienced consequence of eating disorders: isolation from those who love you most. Or as Amy puts it, "the weight of things unsaid."

7. *Wasted* by Marya Hornbacher. The author's honesty and un-willingness to blame others makes this stand out from the horde among addiction memoirs. There's no single reason she turned bulimic at nine and anorexic at fifteen, Hornbacher says. In spite of eccentric parents and frequent moves, her childhood wasn't unhappy; it was "uneasy"—a word that points to her emotional template more than her circumstances. Hornbacher's insights underline a fundamental point: The struggle with food disorders is not about dieting as much as it is about how eating (or not) fills an emotional hole that's hard to climb out of.

8. *Fat: The Anthropology of an Obsession* by Don Kulick and Anne Meneley. These true stories told by thirteen anthropologists and a fat activist force you to remember that *fat* is not a four-letter word everywhere you go. Attitudes toward heavyset people, which change from culture to culture, depend greatly on economic and social factors. Among phat rappers, to be obese is not shameful, but a sign of sexual prowess and economic success. Underground porn aficionados worship Supersize Betty. And in Arab villages in western Niger and neighboring Mauritania, tribes deliberately fatten up girls in early childhood. Where hunger is a threat, padding becomes a symbol of beauty.

9. *Mindless Eating* by Brian Wansink. Stop before you chew again! That's the advice from the head of the Cornell University Food and Brand Lab, who says that our abundance requires the average person to make two hundred food decisions a day. Wansink contends that the road to lasting weight control is to keep track of all that passes your lips, even the mint you downed when you paid the lunch tab. Do you love to eat but lack a greyhound's metabolism? Join the club, Wansink says. Eternal vigilance is the price of peace if you have a well-stocked pantry.

10. *Embracing Your Big Fat Ass* by Laura Banks and Janette Barber. A Big Fat Ass (BFA) is "one of life's biggest jokes, one of its deepest injustices," say these two authors, former stand-up comics, in this book about body image. Fat "is a one-size-fits-all insult," says Rosie O'Donnell in the introduction. To change that conversation, Banks and Barber call themselves B-FABS (Big Fat Ass Babes or Beautiful Fat Ass Babes). They are done with obsessing about their weight. They may still try to take off pounds but won't use it as an excuse for being unhappy. "There is no reason to let your butt be your bane."

THAT MAKE THE MIND/BODY CONNECTION

1. *Sex, Sleep, Eat, Drink, Dream: A Day in the Life of Your Body* by Jennifer Ackerman. "Time is the substance I am made of," wrote Argentine novelist Jorge Borges, and Ackerman devotes an entire book to riffing on this theme. Don't get behind the wheel when you first wake up: It's like driving drunk. Don't reconcile your checkbook in midafternoon: Your brain is on siesta. Okay, make whoopee at night, but testosterone levels are higher in the morning. As for sleep, it's "nature's soft nurse," so allot seven hours. A boatload of research backs up this treasure chest of info about the body's ups and downs.

2. *Woman: An Intimate Geography* by Natalie Angier. Here's science with attitude. In Angier's excursion through the body, she pays special attention to the parts exclusive to the fairer sex, marveling at such miracles as the eye-popping ovary and brain-building breast milk. This go-girl approach leads her to question tired assumptions about a woman's low sex drive and how evolution gave the male a wandering eye. Angier's dukes also go up at the idea that women aren't aggressive: All that separates the sexes on that score, she says, is that women usually pummel opponents with words, not fists.

ANATOMY LESSONS

Consider it one giant leap for womankind: Roughly the same time as American astronauts planted a flag on the moon, a dozen women gathered around a kitchen table in Boston to ask themselves how the burgeoning feminist movement could be adapted to their health and their relationships with their mostly male doctors.

The year was 1969, and a take-back-the-night spirit permeated college campuses (or, at least, women's dorms). By 1970 so, too, did a stapled booklet published by the kitchen-table crowd, which had dubbed itself the Boston Women's Health Book Collective. By 1973, that humble booklet became the full-blown self-help manual *Our Bodies, Ourselves,* notable for its frank approach to sex and reproductive issues.

As a frontline baby boomer, I was among those reading the book's anatomy lessons, including instructions on giving yourself a vaginal examination with a mirror. Frankly, the thought didn't have that much appeal to me. But the way *Our Bodies, Ourselves* argued for a woman's control of her own body caught my attention—and the zeitgeist. It became a bestseller.

The book was bold, and it needed to be. At a time of greater sexual freedom for women, the authors understood what such freedom demanded: knowledge. Without it, women could not make informed decisions about their body or sexual activity. The consequences of ignorance could be serious or even lethal.

Although designed by political activists, not health professionals, *Our Bodies, Ourselves* has become both a symbol of the second-wave women's movement (the first gave us suffrage) as well as a responsible medical guide. The guide remains in print, along with spin-offs that address pregnancy and menopause. It has been adapted or translated into twenty-three languages.

~ Ellen

3. *The Female Brain* by Louann Brizendine. To understand how biology affects a woman's needs and wants, consider the hormones that bathe your mind. Brizendine, a neuropsychiatrist, shows how these chemicals ebb and flow to encourage the mating dance, attention to a child's needs, and a surge of independence when those jobs are done. Biology is not destiny, she declares. Rather, by naming the beast, you control it. Well, maybe not every time, but at least you better understand the maternal urge and other emotions that often hit with no warning.

4. *Blue Beyond Blue: Extraordinary Tales for Ordinary Dilemmas* by Lauren Slater. So much for nature: Let's talk about nurture. That's what psychologist Slater does in these fairy tales, which use storytelling as therapy. Tale number one: A childless woman finds a bird/child and clips off the girl's budding wings to keep her close. Alas, a lover lures her away and encourages her to let her wings sprout. There's a happy ending when the bird/woman empathizes with her mother's dastardly act. "Kindness and cutting, they're all mixed together," she says. Boy, is that the sad truth!

5. *The Spiral Staircase: My Climb Out of Darkness* by Karen Armstrong. In this story about one woman's dark path to self-discovery, Armstrong describes entering and then leaving convent life during the 1960s, and the culture shock that followed. It wasn't just the unfamiliar and sexually liberated world to which she returned. Undiagnosed epilepsy and an emotional flatness made her feel like "a piece of tough steak," incapable of returning even her parents' love. Now a world-renowned scholar,

Armstrong recalls her fight to reclaim hope and the will to go forward when times were tough.

6. *Away: A Novel* by Amy Bloom. Lillian Leyb, Bloom's fictional protagonist, is a lesson in tenacity. In the 1920s, she emigrates from Russia to America after her family is demolished in a pogrom. Yes, she uses sex to survive once she hits the New World, but in a calculating way that depicts the plight of a woman alone. Learning that her young daughter may still be alive in Siberia, she sets off to find her and makes another loop in a life defined by struggle but illuminated with hope and resilience. In the end, Lillian proves that success is best defined not by what happens to you, but how you respond.

7. *A Brief History of Anxiety: Yours and Mine* by Patricia Pearson. Don't panic, but anxiety is the most prevalent mental health problem in the world, with the United States ranking as the most anxious, says Pearson. In less than two hundred pages and with a wit not usually associated with this dour subject, the Toronto-based writer surveys the history of dread—and her own state of paralysis, triggered by such mundane things as the bills and the sight of cows. Pearson replaced drugs and overplanning with cognitive therapy and a dose of old-fashioned faith: "Dare to be irrational." Try this at home, kids.

8. *Wherever You Go, There You Are: Mindfulness Meditation in Everyday Life—10th Anniversary Edition* by Jon Kabat-Zinn. Here's another antidote to anxiety that Pearson and thousands of other nervous wrecks have found useful: meditation. Once seen

as an exotic Eastern practice, Kabat-Zinn helped popularize mindfulness in the West by publishing the first accessible guide to the practice in 1994. Peppering his text with quotes from Thoreau, Whitman, and Lao-Tzu, the expert on stress reduction offers practical advice for slowing down the pace: "Just sit. Reside at the center of the world. Let things be as they are."

9. *Out of Her Mind: Women Writing on Madness* edited by Rebecca Shannonhouse. Was Zelda Fitzgerald destined to be mentally ill or was she driven mad by a stifling marriage? In her anthology of fiction and nonfiction about women's emotional suffering, Shannonhouse raises this and other sticky questions— "big, eternal ones about the meaning of insanity." Some of her choices are classics: Charlotte Perkins Gilman's 1892 short story "The Yellow Wallpaper," written when women were diagnosed with "hysteria." Others, like filmmaker Allie Light's "Thorazine Shuffle" on how prescription drugs affect your personality, are more modern, but no less terrifying.

10. *Exuberance: The Passion for Life* by Kay Redfield Jamison. After chronicling her own manic depression in *An Unquiet Mind*, psychiatry professor Jamison turns to a subject often overlooked by her psychosis-obsessed field: unfettered joy. Exuberance can turn to mania, but more often it is the catalyst to an extraordinarily rich life, she says in this effusive exploration on all things exuberant, including Walt Whitman, John Philip Sousa, jazz, square dancing, rock and roll, Chuck Yeager, Ted Turner, P. T. Barnum, *Oklahoma!*, Louis Armstrong, and Theodore Roosevelt. "A passion for life is life's ultimate affirmation," she concludes.

THAT STALK THE DIVINE

1. *In the Spirit of Happiness: A Book of Spiritual Wisdom* by the Monks of New Skete. A cloistered community of Greek Orthodox monks known best for raising German shepherds may seem to share few of the concerns that color a woman's life. Not so! The discipline required for spiritual growth and authentic happiness is universal. When prayer leaves you cold or someone drives you nuts, don't give up, they say; instead, practice love. Even small acts contain the seeds of transformation. "Wandering through the dark isn't pleasant," Father Laurance says, "but if you're patient, your eyes adjust."

2. *Gilead* by Marilynne Robinson. Life with all its blessings and crises takes glorious form in this story told by a fictional small-town preacher. Realizing his days are numbered, the elderly Reverend John Ames offers his young son this legacy: his tale of growing up in the heartland, serving as God's emissary, and receiving a woman's love. Wisdom flows from the page as he talks about discovering passion late in life: "I might seem to be comparing something great and holy with a minor and ordinary thing, that is, love of God with mortal love. But I just don't see them as separate things at all."

3. *The Places That Scare You: A Guide to Fearlessness in Difficult Times* by Pema Chodron. As the old saying goes, change is the

WORKOUTS FOR THE SOUL

Call me a Christian guideposts junkie. When I was young, I read the inspirational column that ran in the newspaper each day during Lent. Now I subscribe to the daily Scripture reading from Beliefnet.com and browse regularly through the short shelf of daily meditation books above my bed. I'm not alone: The habit of daily meditation seems to be on the rise, fueled by the faithful, the hassled, and grads of the recovery movement.

Books that feature Bible-based readings are big. But so, too, are ones that define wisdom in nonreligious terms, like *Meditations for Women Who Do Too Much*. The main idea is to take a moment out of your day to reflect on how you spend it and why.

Perhaps no one took this practice more seriously than Leo Tolstoy. In 1902, at age seventy-five, the Russian writer nearly died from pneumonia and typhoid fever. While recuperating, he meditated daily on a nugget of wisdom drawn from his voluminous reading. (It's not hard to find material when your personal library contains more than twenty-two thousand volumes.) Convinced that such daily reflections made sense for everyone, he subsequently published three collections containing a range of thought-provoking passages, from the words of great writers to aphorisms like "God lives in every kind person." His daily workout for the soul took readers through the calendar year with tidbits on such topics as the soul, faith, and love.

A contemporary writer who also has spiritual matters on her mind is Madeleine L'Engle, who's known best for her children's books (*A Wrinkle in Time*). Snippets of her fiction and nonfiction are captured in one of my favorite guides, *Glimpses of Grace: Daily Thoughts and Reflections*, written with Presbyterian minister Carole F. Chase.

From her September 27 entry: "Does enjoying my faith imply protection from the slings and arrows of outrageous fortune? No. It did not stop my husband from dying prematurely. It did not stop a careless truck driver from going through a red light and nearly killing me. My faith is not a magic charm, like garlic to chase away vampires. It is, instead, what sustains me in the midst of all the normal joys and tragedies of the normal human life."

~ Ellen

one thing you can count on. Yield to it, says Chodron, a Buddhist nun, whose recipe for happiness employs a concept her religion calls *tonglen,* which translates as exchanging yourself for others. In true Buddhist fashion, God is not apparent, but the route to spiritual growth is obvious: Embrace the dynamic quality of the universe, go with the flow, and prepare yourself for the peace that passes understanding when you move forward without fear.

4. *Dakota: A Spiritual Geography* by Kathleen Norris. "For me, walking in a hard Dakota wind can be like staring at the ocean: humbled before its immensity, I also have a sense of being at home on this planet," writes Norris, a poet, who left New York City for an isolated part of the Midwest to reclaim her family home. This evocative memoir tells about finding herself, her faith, and a sense of community in this windswept spot. Her best spiritual lesson is wrung from living in a small town: "Gossip is theology translated into experience."

5. *Stalking the Divine* by Kristin Ohlson. Ohlson was a doubter when she hit midlife and suddenly felt the impulse to return to her Catholic faith. "I wanted a steadying hope after my twenty-two-year marriage had ended, after this new one had begun, after my children had the audacity to grow up and my parents had the audacity to grow old, after I sensed that whatever I thought I knew of the world wasn't enough." With similar directness, her memoir describes how an inner-city parish and a group of cloistered nuns gave her ballast and a new understanding of God.

6. *A Prayer for Owen Meany* by John Irving. You can read this novel in more than one way: as satire, or—and this is the Babes' way—as a deeper dive into the mystery of faith. Owen Meany, a diminutive oddball who grows up in a small New Hampshire town believing he's God's instrument, makes a believer out of the book's narrator, John Wheelwright. In this story about love, death, Vietnam, and learning to live in an imperfect world, Owen teaches John to believe, but with a caveat: "Watch out for people who call themselves religious—make sure they know what they mean."

7. *The Gospel According to Sydney Welles* by Susi Rajah. Looking for God in an ad agency may seem a bit unorthodox, but Sydney Welles is desperate. She's just landed an unusual client—the Catholic Church—and her own life is in shambles. Why not seek divine intervention? In her debut novel, Rajah makes us laugh and think about the ultimate meaning of life, especially when Welles e-mails God (at such imaginative URLs as God c/o info@godmademedoit.net): "If you had intended us to solve the mystery of existence, you'd have made us a lot smarter."

8. *The Life of Pi* by Yann Martel. In this novel, Piscine Patel (nickname Pi) is so interested in religion he becomes a Hindu, Muslim, *and* a Christian. He also studies zoology. When he's stranded in a lifeboat with a tiger, he uses both science and religion to survive. But was there ever really a tiger in his lifeboat? When Pi offers two versions of his shipwreck adventure, he leaves it to you to decide whether you prefer the story with the animal. And so it goes with believing in God, says Pi.

9. *When Bad Things Happen to Good People* by Harold S. Kushner. When Kushner's three-year-old son was diagnosed with a degenerative disease, the rabbi not only was heartbroken; he found his faith sorely tested: How could God do this to me? After Aaron died in his teens, Kushner tried—for himself and for others—to sort out how to hold on to faith in a world of suffering. He approaches the dilemma with a father's aching heart and a rabbi's soulfulness. His conclusion? "To live fully, bravely, and meaningfully in this less-than-perfect world," God gives you two weapons: "the ability to forgive and the ability to love."

10. The Illustrated Edition of *Care of the Soul: How to Add Depth and Meaning to Your Everyday Life* by Thomas Moore. Spiritual life shouldn't be practiced only in a church pew. To feed your soul, you need to tap into the sacred of everyday life—for example, in a garden or in a painting, says Moore, an art therapist and former Catholic monk, in this inspiring combination of text

and illustrations. Even the reverie induced by the ritual of washing and drying dishes can be an occasion for soul work, he says. "The soul is to be found in the oddest places."

THAT TAP YOUR INNER ARTIST

1. *The Artist's Way: A Spiritual Path to Creativity* by Julia Cameron. This book helped coin the term *inner artist* and remains a classic hands-on advice book for finding your creative self. Cameron defines creativity in such broad terms that anyone can apply. A former problem drinker, she offers a twelve-week (like twelve-step, get it?) program that includes using a daily journal to record your inner thoughts. You don't need special talent, just the ability to set aside time and believe that what you're doing is serious business—for your soul, if not your pocketbook.

2. *Writing Down the Bones: Freeing the Writer Within* by Natalie Goldberg. As long as we're on the subject of classics, hie yourself to the bookstore for this little treasure, first published in 1986. It starts with the same premise as Cameron's: Don't self-censor. Sit down to write the same way you'd go out for a jog, without expecting to break some world record. Then drink in her down-home advice about learning how to listen ("send" mode is a tough way to find material), adding the significant detail, and exploring the subjects closest to your heart.

3. *Proust Was a Neuroscientist* by Jonah Lehrer. Lehrer isn't the first writer to make the case for how artists intuit what scientists quantify. Virginia Woolf's *To the Lighthouse* offered a blueprint for later research on brain hemispheres, he says, and Gertrude Stein's "rose is a rose" anticipated linguist Noam Chomsky. By putting artists on top for a change, Lehrer argues that progress requires the imagination as much as it does the scientific method. As Proust put it, "The impression is for the writer what experimentation is for the scientist."

4. *Einstein's Dreams* by Alan Lightman. Even scientists need imagination to spark new discoveries, as Lightman cleverly demonstrates in his re-creation of the dreams that a patent clerk named Albert Einstein might have had while working on his theory about the nature of time. In one dream, time is a circle, bending back on itself. In another, it slows down at high altitudes (people build houses on mountaintops to stay young). Lightman's fanciful novel is a delight to read—and a painless way to learn how important intuition is to science.

5. *Savage Beauty: The Life of Edna St. Vincent Millay* by Nancy Milford. We love *Zelda*, Milford's biography of F. Scott Fitzgerald's ill-fated wife. But this biography by the same author about a more successful woman writer might give you hope instead of despair. As the first woman to win a Pulitzer Prize for poetry, Millay scored high on the literary Richter scale. She transcended her problematic background with talent and moxie. But her ecstatic nature, a mommy fetish, and huge ambition show life and art can be precarious, even at the top.

6. *The Creative Habit: Learn It and Use It For Life* by Twyla Tharp. "Creativity is not just for artists," says Tharp. Business-people, engineers, and parents trying to inspire their children also need to see the world in more than one way. To help, Tharp offers this book of exercises, both physical and mental, sprinkled with sage advice: Create a starting ritual. Make lists. Put the name of your project down. Don't forget there's an *A* in *failure*. Tharp claims it took her 128 ballets to feel like a master choreographer. By that time she was fifty-eight.

7. *Twenty-eight Artists and Two Saints: Essays* by Joan Acocella. What makes an artist? Judging by Acocella's lively essays, not necessarily an unhappy childhood. More important is tenacity and the ability to accept disappointment, says the *New Yorker* critic. And, often, sheer luck. Among those bucking up under adversity are choreographers Tharp and Martha Graham, sculptor Louise Bourgeois, writers Penelope Fitzgerald and Dorothy Parker (and saints Mary Magdalene and Joan of Arc). Acocella does include a few anomalies, like Susan Sontag, whose career was not marked by hardship. "It is nice to know that somebody got a break."

8. *Notes on the Need for Beauty: An Intimate Look at an Essential Quality* by J. Ruth Gendler. "Sight leads to insight," says Gendler, whose book offers a meditation for the creative mind. Art has always been linked to beauty, but what is beautiful? Gendler, a visual artist, doesn't settle for one definition in this lyrical exploration of the subject. Instead, she embraces the paradox of a quality so elusive it can be found in both junkyards and sunsets. "Beauty rinses our eyes," says Gendler, whose own whimsical line drawings accompany the text.

9. *Sleeping with Schubert* by Bonnie Marson. This titillating plot shouldn't work, but it does: Franz Schubert—yes, the nineteenth century composer of the *Unfinished Symphony*—invades the body of Brooklyn lawyer Liza Durbin while the latter is shopping at Nordstrom. It works because Marson peoples her seriocomic novel with just the right balance of wacky and realistic characters. But even if you don't buy the admittedly bizarre premise, Marson's story of unfinished business can provide you a rare glimpse into what inspires musicians (Schubert, via Durbin, begins to compose again). Can't you just hear the movie soundtrack?

10. *Letters to a Young Poet* by Rainer Maria Rilke. There are easier ways to tap into your inner artist than being inhabited by a dead composer. Franz Kappus found an inspirational mentor simply by sending his poems to one of the most celebrated poets of his day, asking him to comment on his verse. Over the next five years, from 1903–1908, Rilke corresponded with the young poet, commiserating with the sensitive man's struggles with solitude, faith, and love. You don't have to be a wannabe poet to profit from the sound advice Rilke gave him: Stop looking for affirmation from others. Find it in yourself.

IV

FAMILY & FRIENDS

Tolstoy wrote, "All happy families resemble one another, each unhappy family is unhappy in its own way."

The Babes say, Baloney. Sure, this line has literary resonance—perfect for the beginning of the Russian writer's grand novel *Anna Karenina,* about a woman who betrays her husband for love. But it doesn't stack up in real life.

Test the thesis with your own kin: In which of those neat packages, happy or unhappy, do yours belong? Probably neither. Any family comes with multiple members and weather systems that vary, depending on events and emotional inclinations. The "family," defined either as the few clustered under one roof or the many connected by blood ties, is such a dynamic social system that—to paraphrase a favorite *Seinfeld* episode—just one psychiatrist couldn't do the trick. A whole team of Viennese psychiatrists is needed to parse this one out.

Not that you can't try.

In this section, the Babes put family relationships under the microscope. Friends and furry creatures figure in (realizing, of course, that sometimes either or both often serve as family substitutes).

But relatives elbow their way to the center because no matter where you look—fiction, self-help, memoir—they keep coming up. Especially in this day of variations that include step-, blended, adopted, interracial, and so on, family is the octopus with more tentacles than you can count.

A social worker might say that this attention makes sense because the family is the building block of society. But don't expect such a clinical interpretation from us: The books we recommend are tuned to the heartstrings. All speak to the improbable truth that parents and children and siblings bind like glue to your psyche even when you don't want them to.

You get to choose your friends and your pets. That's why they sometimes serve as such refuges in the storm, as companions and mother confessors. But this underlines the point that literature pounds home time and again: Love 'em or leave 'em, family is hard to shake.

This explains why, long before Gregory Mendel started fiddling with peapods and—eureka—unlocked the key to genetics, the Greeks made cathartic drama from the ties that bind. It explains why Freud borrowed from the toga crowd to name our neuroses (Oedipal complex and so forth). It explains why the family is the gift that keeps on giving to shrinks—and to writers.

So let's give Tolstoy's famous line its due. If you're going to tell stories about family, which kind works better, happy or unhappy? The playwright Aeschylus pointed the way from Athens circa 500 B.C.E.

His House of Atreus features a family in which father sacrifices daughter, mother kills father, daughter talks brother into killing mother—and, with all that, who needs to get into the uncle who was tricked into eating his children? The crown of guilt rests on the son's head and the family line goes forward, cursed.

In all likelihood, these circumstances aren't repeating themselves in your household. But in order to make good drama, Aeschylus—as well as modern tragedians Eugene O'Neill and Edward Albee, to name two—turned small stones into huge boulders, metaphorically speaking. Audiences are mesmerized by the staging of stories that flip devotion on its back and show the betrayal and rage on its dark underbelly.

Nobel Prize–winner Doris Lessing, with a writer's ear for such impulses, says that anger against her own mother inspired her first novel, *Martha Quest,* which includes an epic mother-daughter battle scene. Downsizing these feelings to a manageable size, she recalls in her latest book, *Alfred and Emily*, the true-life tale of an actress who returned to the stage after several years at home with her daughter.

The actress brought the young girl to see her perform, and afterward, a friend asked innocently enough, "Didn't you feel proud to see your mother up there?"

The question, Lessing reports, released an unexpected outburst. "Her? Oh, she wasn't anything, she wasn't much, she isn't anything really," the daughter replied.

The mother's decision to sacrifice time with her daughter in order to resume her stage career put a small tear in the fabric of maternal love—small enough, you hope, that it will mend, and mom and child will adjust to the necessary and normal process of letting go. But sometimes the break is wrenching.

In her essay "Navigating the Channel Islands," novelist Jo-Ann Mapson recalls the recriminations and second chances that marked her relationship with her adolescent son. She didn't give up when he stole her wedding ring. But after he started college, he overdrew his bank account and kept taking advantage of his parents. Finally, Mapson and her husband gave up.

"His bedroom has been made anonymous with redecorating, but I still rarely go there. Every morning I awaken with pain in my chest, a solid weight I've learned to carry. I get up and go to the computer, where I sit alone and write stories about hope and the power of love, trying not collapse under the irony of such claims. Some days it's harder than others to locate that thread of possibility."

Mapson recalls her grateful tears when her son was born and contrasts them with the way they sting now. Her poignant essay sums up the yin and yang of family life, which produces such strong feelings that the potential for joy or heartbreak are always juxtaposed.

Poet Jane Shore uses Tolstoy's famous line ironically in the title of her book *Happy Family*—not to claim the truth of what he said, but to show how much more complicated matters are than "happy" or "sad." Whatever the emotional temperature, the bond is as obvious as her eyes, nose, and mouth, she contends:

Now, at fifty,
I stare into her mirror
  glazed with our common face,
the face I'll pass down to my daughter
  who I sometimes see watching from behind me
  with the same puzzled look I had

when I watched my mother,
out of the corner of her eye,
watching me.

FOR MAKING PEACE WITH MOM

1. *Circling My Mother* by Mary Gordon. Although better known for writing about her father and his secrets in *Shadow Man*, Gordon has also written a memoir about her Catholic, working-class mother, beginning with the last years of her life, "marked by dementia, when she was much more a problem to me than a joy." Gordon looks at Anna's ninety-four years of life from many points, "only one of which was her career as my mother." Her love of music. Her four sisters. Her friends and faith. Her polio and her drinking. Her marriage. What emerges is a vivid mosaic that takes on a life of its own: "She has become my words."

2. *The Light of Evening* by Edna O'Brien. This novel from one of Ireland's best writers (there are so many) explores the plight of mothers and daughters who love each other but never feel like kindred souls. Dilly, the mom, is desperate to stay connected with Eleanora, the child who traces their estrangement to the time she refused to take Communion and was badgered by her mother: "Why, why, my young lady." A mother's need to hold on and a daughter's need for freedom will always clash, but in the final scene a quiet togetherness closes the breach, at least for a moment.

3. *Motherless Daughters: The Legacy of Loss* by Hope Edelman. Edelman, who lost her mother to breast cancer when she was seventeen, hit a chord with this book, which was first published in 1994. Haunted by how her adolescent rebellion dovetailed with her mother's death, Edelman wonders what could have been: "Would we have had time to become friends?" She explores other women's experiences and concludes that mother loss is traumatic at any stage. But the legacy remains. "Our lives are shaped as much by those who leave us as they are by those who stay."

4. *Eva Moves the Furniture* by Margot Livesey. Here's a fictional soul mate to Edelman's subject: After Eva McEwen's mother dies at her birth, the Scottish girl grows up with two angels at her shoulder—imaginary (or are they?) companions who join her on her motherless journey through life. When illness strikes Eva, her young daughter, Ruth, begs her not to go away. "I promise, but you may not always know that I'm keeping my promise," Eva tells her. Better than a Ouija board, this magical novel evokes the presence of lost loved ones among us.

5. *I Am My Mother's Daughter: Making Peace With Mom Before It's Too Late* by Iris Krasnow. "Stop crying. Everyone dies," Krasnow's mother, a Holocaust survivor, snapped when her six-year-old daughter mourned the death of a family friend. It wasn't easy to have a mom this tough, but Krasnow's point is that you don't get to choose, so forgive even if you can't forget. Drawing from her own experiences and a host of interviews, the journalist contrasts a child's resentment with an adult perspective that measures moms according to their devotion, not their personality flaws.

6. *Secret Daughter: A Mixed-Race Daughter and the Mother Who Gave Her Away* by June Cross. Cross, whose father was black, could have been angry with the white mother who pretended they weren't related and let another couple raise her. Instead, she uses her journalistic skills to gain distance and chalk up her mother's inadequacies as a parent to a poor upbringing and racial bigotry beyond her control. After convincing her mother to acknowledge their relationship publicly, the adult Cross tries to shelve the pain of the past, telling her mom, "You did the best you could."

7. *Let Me Go* by Helga Schneider. Schneider can neither forgive nor forget. When she was four, her mother abandoned the family to join the SS and work at a Nazi concentration camp. In 1998, Schneider paid call in order to bear final witness to her mother's deeds and her own horror that "this woman lives within me." Her record of their encounter shows an old woman who still clings to Nazi ideology and a daughter equally determined to force her to confront her collaboration with evil.

8. *The Joy Luck Club* by Amy Tan. Mother and daughter relationships are often difficult, but when the clash of cultures is added to the clash of generations, things really get sticky, as Tan demonstrates in her classic tale of four China-born mothers—members of the mah-jongg-playing Joy Luck Club—struggling to understand their American-born daughters. Love mingles with confusion, guilt with anger for mothers and daughters alike. "Oh, her strength! her weakness!—both pulling me apart," says daughter Waverly Jong. "My mind was flying one way, my heart another."

9. *Possessing the Secret of Joy* by Alice Walker. Tashi, a minor character in Walker's novel *The Color Purple,* reappears in this searing story. Unable to get over the pain of the ritual circumcision she was subjected to during her childhood in Africa, she returns to her Olinkan village to exact revenge. She doesn't lash out at her mother, who like countless women before her was a silent accomplice to this mutilation—why blame another victim?—but at the midwife who oversaw the operation. How can you possess the secret of joy? Resistance.

10. *West of Then* by Tara Bray Smith. Here's a poignant twist on the typical mother-daughter relationship. Tara Bray Smith's mother, a descendant of Hawaiian plantation owners and a heroin addict, left her daughter to be raised by the child's father when Smith was seven. Twenty-five years later, Smith receives a call from that absent mom. She's living on the streets of Honolulu. In this moving memoir, a daughter describes her search for her hapless mother, caught in the incongruity of homelessness in paradise. "I don't know why I think my mother is my responsibility, but I do."

FOR DEALING WITH DAD

1. *A Thousand Acres* by Jane Smiley. It's no secret that this story of a dominating father who cuts one of his three daughters out of his thousand-acre estate is based on *King Lear.* Its theme of madness matches the darkness of the Bard's royal tale (adding incest, to up the ante). But don't worry. You don't have to be a scholar to appreciate this feminist twist on an old story of fatherly favoritism. Smiley's detailed description of farm life and the hauntingly flat landscape of Iowa will dispel any anxieties left over from Lit 101.

2. *American Pastoral* by Philip Roth. Jewish golden-boy "Swede" Levov's version of paradise is blasted to smithereens when his stuttering sixteen-year-old daughter sets off a murderous bomb to protest the Vietnam War. The violence "transports him out of the longed-for American pastoral and into . . . the indigenous American berserk," writes Roth in this absorbing novel of generational conflict. Like the country, Levov is awakened to the "horror of self-reflection." Who or what is to blame? His sexual peccadilloes? Outside agitators? Or the inevitable gulf between daughters who think too much and fathers who think too little?

3. *Brother, I'm Dying* by Edwidge Danticat. One brother left; the other remained. Novelist Danticat contrasts her immigrant father with his priest brother, who stayed in their native Haiti, as she weaves together a very personal story of life and death, separation and sacrifice. Danticat was raised by both men because her parents had to wait eight years to bring her and her brother to join them in the United States. Asked if he's had a happy life, Danticat's ailing father replies, "You, my children, have not shamed me." Quite an understatement, in light of the writer's ability to evoke his humility and courage.

4. *The Historian* by Elizabeth Kostova. "This is the story of how as a girl of sixteen I went in search of my father and his past," writes the historian who narrates this modern-day twist on the age-old vampire myth. This daughter's search takes her from a library in Oxford to an archive in Istanbul and a ruined monastery in Transylvania. There she tracks down the story of Vlad the Impaler, whose bloody regime gave rise to the Dracula legend. Not interested in vampires? Kostova's heart-racing prose will win you over. She's that good.

5. *One Drop: My Father's Secret Life: A Story of Race and Family Secrets* by Bliss Broyard. In this gutsy memoir, Broyard lays bare the nation's mind-boggling way of categorizing race through the story of her father's decision to hide his black ancestry. Tracking down her Creole past from New Orleans to California, Bliss doesn't shy away from the ugly aspects of critic Anatole Broyard's choice, including shunning his own dark-skinned mother and sister. "To reveal the young colored boy that my father had been, I had to carefully strip away the father that I had known."

6. *House of Happy Endings* by Leslie Garis. It sounds so romantic— the large, handsome abode called the Dell, where Garis grew up with grandparents who were both noted children's writers. But appearances (and titles) can be deceiving. In this memoir, Garis focuses on her tormented father, also a writer, but one who feels smothered by the success of parents who created such adored childhood companions as Uncle Wiggily and the Bobbsey Twins. Garis's regret is less for his failed career than his inability to appreciate how much he was loved.

7. *Fun Home: A Family Tragicomic* by Alison Bechdel. *Six Feet Under* meets *The Addams Family* in this memoir, which combines gothic drawings and a seductive text. Bechdel delivers laugh-out-loud stories of the family's funeral business ("The Fun Home"), her father's obsession with interior decorating, and her own coming out as a lesbian. She also confronts with disarming honesty her father's ambiguous sexuality and death: "Perhaps my eagerness to claim him as 'gay' in the way I am 'gay' as opposed to bisexual . . . is just a way of keeping him to myself . . . a sort of inverted Oedipal complex."

8. *Disgrace* by J. M. Coetzee. Professor David Lurie, the leading man in this prize-winning novel about South Africa, is a lecherous old goat who gets chased away from his academic post on sexual-harassment charges. He decamps to his daughter's place in the country, where his views on almost everything, including women, are challenged after a violent attack. Lurie's trauma as he struggles to understand his daughter serves as a metaphor for the political and social upheavals in his country. You may never like him, but you'll appreciate how his daughter disrupts his complacency.

9. *Dress Codes: Of Three Girlhoods—My Mother's, My Father's, and Mine* by Noelle Howey. Her father was Dick. Now he's Christine. This memoir charts the evolution that led him/her from cross-dressing to a sex-change operation to a final, head-spinning coming out as a lesbian. To say this took its toll on Howey and her family is to put it mildly. But she lets you laugh at the absurdity of it all even while feeling her pain. Skip the violins: "I am a different person because my father was a man, then a girl, then a woman," she writes. Still, "This isn't tragedy. It's just non-fiction."

10. *The Middle Place* by Kelly Corrigan. "The thing you need to know about me is that I'm George Corrigan's daughter, his only daughter." So begins this sweet account of a father and daughter who simultaneously battled cancer—breast for her, bladder for him. Corrigan, a wife, mother, and newspaper columnist, leaves little doubt that her eternally upbeat dad helped them both through their respective fights. "People walk away from him feeling like they're on their game, even if they suspect that he put them there," she says. It's hard to resist a man whose "default setting is open delight."

ABOUT SIBLINGS, WITH OR WITHOUT RIVALRY

1. *Having Our Say: The Delany Sisters' First 100 Years* by Sarah and A. Elizabeth Delany with Amy Hill Hearth. The Delanys have had a long time to work out sibling rivalries. Daughters of a former slave and members of a prominent black family, the college-educated sisters lived together most of their lives. At 103 and 101, still living on their own, they wrote this witty memoir. Bessie: "People learned not to mess with me from Day One." Sadie: "The way I see it, there's room in the world for both me and Bessie. We kind of balance each other out."

2. *The Rare and the Beautiful: The Art, Love and Lives of the Garman Sisters* by Cressida Connolly. Juicy literary gossip abounds in this account of the exploits of the Garman sisters and (despite this title) their brother, who dazzled London art circles in the mid-twentieth century. Mary dallied with Vita Sackville-West (replacing a miffed Virginia Woolf); Kathleen bedded sculptor Joseph Epstein (and was shot by his jealous wife); Lorna posed for and slept with painter Lucian Freud; Douglas moved in with heiress Peggy Guggenheim. An admirer: "The Garmans changed people's lives. Most people weren't used to having their reality enhanced like that."

3. *Rise and Shine* by Anna Quindlen. In this novel from a prize-winning columnist, the stars are Meghan Fitzmaurice, who anchors the nation's most watched morning TV show, and her younger sister, Bridget, a low-key, faithful sidekick. Each knows her place until Meghan's career and marriage take a sudden nose-dive and Bridget is shocked to see flaws in their sisterly arrangement. Quindlen takes a cut at both the superficial glitter of celebrity and its pressures. Bridget is so content basking in her sister's glow that she doesn't notice the pressure building up until the top blows off. Ouch.

4. *The Doctor's House* by Ann Beattie. Dysfunction junction at the top binds siblings more than anything. In this novel, an odd bro-and-sis relationship stems from maternal neglect and a father's philandering. As adults, Nina and Andrew can't seem to recalibrate their codependence: Nina plays room monitor to Andrew's playboy antics, deploring his irresponsibility while living vicariously through his exploits. Looking at this troubled tribe from different perspectives, Beattie uses fiction to plumb the souls of the self-involved and find the roots for their selfishness.

5. *Body Surfing* by Anita Shreve. In this deceptively light novel set at a cottage on the shores of New Hampshire, three siblings vie for the attention of Sydney Sklar, who has been hired for the summer to tutor the youngest, the sensitive and "slow" Julie. Sydney's presence attracts the interest of Julie's two older brothers, who take a break from their jobs to vacation with their family. A divorcee and a widow, the already fragile Sydney is nearly destroyed by a fraternal competition she discovers too late.

6. *Hilary and Jackie: The True Story of Two Sisters Who Shared a Passion, a Madness and a Man* by Hilary du Pre and Piers du Pre. Artistic geniuses aren't always easy to get along with. In fact, their talent sometimes gives them license to act in untenable ways. This seems to have been the case with British cellist Jacqueline du Pre, who died at forty from multiple sclerosis. Hilary—known to Jackie as "Bar"—recalls taking second seat to her sister in childhood and then later watching as Jackie made a play for her husband. For Hilary, sisterly love endured, but with her guard up.

7. *The Vanishing Act of Esme Lennox* by Maggie O'Farrell. Iris Lockhart had never heard of Esme Lennox, even though she is her grandmother's sister. When she's called to take charge of her, she befriends the old woman and pieces together her story, uncovering an act of sisterly betrayal so cruel that it would seem impossible if not for extenuating circumstances. The odd chemistry between Iris and her stepbrother further complicates a novel that shows how the sins of one generation can play havoc with the next.

8. *Identical Strangers: A Memoir of Twins Separated and Reunited* by Elyse Schein and Paula Bernstein. At the age of thirty-five, the authors discover that they are identical twins, each distributed to a different adoptive family as part of an ethically challenged study on nature versus nurture. This joint memoir recollects two lives lived separately and reports the latest in twin research, much of which shows Mother Nature with an upper hand.

9. *My Sister's Keeper* by Jodi Picoult. Imagine that your parents conceived you only to be a donor for your ailing sibling. That's the intriguing premise of this thought-provoking novel. Anna Fitzgerald has given an umbilical cord, blood, and bone marrow to her sister, Kate, who has a rare form of leukemia. When her sister needs a liver, thirteen-year-old Anna balks. She hires a lawyer to sue her parents for the right to make her own decisions about her body, raising important ethical questions about genetic engineering, but also about the true nature of sisterly love.

10. *Night of Many Dreams* by Gail Tsukiyama. Talk about cheese and chalk. Joan and Emma Lew, two sisters growing up in Hong Kong during and after World War II, are opposites: Joan is such a beauty that her mother plots her marriage prospects over mah-jongg, while the younger Emma solemnly accepts her role as the industrious but plain go-along. But fate has a way of superseding Mah-Mee's intentions, and Auntie Go, who runs a business instead of a household, makes new options possible. Females rule the roost in a novel that shows life is messy, but family is constant.

ABOUT FAMILIES MORE DYSFUNCTIONAL THAN YOURS

1. *The Corrections* by Jonathan Franzen. As Franzen's fictional brood demonstrates, there's nothing like family to drive you crazy. Alfred and Enid still battle each other in their overstuffed home in St. Jude, a Midwestern suburb; their three grown-up offspring, transplanted to the Northeast, are disappointments to their parents and to themselves. But, like stock market corrections that only seriously hurt "fools and the working poor," the well-heeled Lamberts adjust as the once-dominant Alfred descends into dementia and they slouch toward "one last Christmas" together. St. Jude, after all, is the patron saint of hopeless and desperate cases.

2. *Housekeeping* by Marilynne Robinson. Ruth and Lucille's father deserted them, their mother died after driving into a lake, and now they're living in the chaotic household of their mother's unconventional sister Sylvie. But Robinson's classic novel, written with the intensity of a poem, does not prove the transience of love. Quite the contrary. When Lucille bails out for a more structured life and narrator Ruth sets off with her vagabond aunt

FORTUNE AND FRAUD:
TALES OF AN UNHAPPY CHILDHOOD

The memoir as a literary form can be traced back to Augustine's *Confessions*, written about 400 A.D. But the modern boom in memoirs found its guiding lights in writers such as Frank Conroy (*Stop-Time*, 1977) and Tobias Wolff (*This Boy's Life*, 1988, featured in 10 to Help You Think Like a Guy), who both turned bittersweet childhoods into great copy.

In the mid-nineties Mary Karr pushed the memoir about unhappy childhood to center stage with her best seller, *The Liars' Club* (see number 7). Suddenly, it seemed as if everyone was writing about their odd or tragic background. Real-life stories about sad pasts, written like fiction: If you wrote one, the readers would come.

Fast-forward a decade, however, and you see this formula stumbling on its own excess. First James Frey received a public shaming from Oprah Winfrey for exaggerating his tale of addiction and recovery in *A Million Little Pieces*. Then Margaret B. Jones got caught making up the entire story that was supposed to be her own in *Love and Consequences*.

My sense is that these examples of authorial overkill are a good sign: It means that the wave of woe has crested, and the memoir genre must mature in new directions.

At the least, the frauds help readers see how the literary memoir ought to work. Facts are stubborn things, so if an author can't stick to them, her book should be called what it is—fiction. Emotional truth is something else, however. That's how the author experienced what happened, and how honestly that is depicted is something only the writer knows for sure.

~ Ellen

into the darkness, Robinson's theme, with its echoes of the biblical story of Martha and Mary, becomes clear: Good housekeeping is not the only sign of love.

3. *We Were the Mulvaneys* by Joyce Carol Oates. Newspaperman Judd Mulvaney narrates this novel about his once-picture-perfect family. Ensconced on an idyllic farm and operating a prosperous small business in upstate New York, the Mulvaneys are living the American dream until sixteen-year-old Marianne is raped. The event sets off a chain reaction that destroys not just the family, but also their shared belief that theirs was a family "in which everything that happened to them was precious." Oates, a master of digging into the underbelly of families and their secrets, celebrates family ties while demonstrating their fragility.

4. *The Gathering* by Anne Enright. "God, I hate my family, these people I never chose to love, but love all the same." Veronica, this novel's narrator, has good reason for contradictory feelings about her Irish clan: Brother Liam, the family black sheep, has just committed suicide. In the shadow of that loss, her mind spins backward to their life together and a secret that's key to her brother's sad ending. In this story about a sister's grief and guilt, Enright draws a convincing portrait—a family portrait, no less—of how devotion and sorrow are inseparable.

5. *Bad Blood* by Lorna Sage. Grandparents also play a role in this British writer's sharp-eyed memoir of growing up in three troubled households. Her mother's parents were a philandering parish priest and his angry, pagan wife. Her own parents were less mismatched than totally inept. And then comes Sage's own shotgun wedding at age sixteen. A love of learning ends her story with a twist as Sage, a noted critic, describes how she and her husband "broke the rules and got away with it."

6. *Sweet and Low* by Rich Cohen. Revenge is a dish best served cold, and Cohen, whose mother "and her issue" were cut out of her family's estate, serves up a hearty plateful. The grandson of the inventor of the Sweet'N Low fortune inherited a rollicking good story, though, peopled with some of the most eccentric family members since *Cat on a Hot Tin Roof,* including Aunt Gladys, who never leaves her refrigerated bedroom, and Uncle Martin, indicted on federal charges. An added bonus: You'll learn a lot about Brooklyn and the saccharine sweetener industry, pink packets and all.

7. *The Liars' Club* by Mary Karr. Poet Karr, a pioneer of the literary confessional genre, apparently inherited the ability to tell a story from her yarn-spinning dad. This classic shows how an unstable childhood colors self-perception, so that "the fact that my house was Not Right metastasized into the notion that I myself was Not Right," with constant vigilance against "Not-Rightness" required. She doesn't play the blame game, though: Karr is kind toward her troubled mom and shows how humor and resilience sifted down amid the chaos.

8. *The Glass Castle* by Jeannette Walls. Another standout in the "loser family" sweepstakes is this account of Walls's childhood.

With a mom and dad whose delusions made them a perfect match, she and her three siblings were nomads growing up penniless and on the lam. When landlords or the law got fussy, she recalls, "we were always doing the skedaddle." When the cupboard was bare, her mother just shrugged. Amazingly, all four children transcended this upbringing—maybe because the one thing their parents didn't scrimp on was a belief in themselves and the kids they neglected so badly.

9. *Prince of Tides* by Pat Conroy. The granddaddy of dysfunctional-family novels, moving from the low country of South Carolina to Manhattan, tells the devastating impact of family abuse. Encouraged by a psychiatrist who is treating his twin sister after her attempted suicide, narrator Tom Wingo recounts the details of their traumatic childhood, marked by the violence of an abusive father and the passive-aggressiveness of a mother who is both victim and victimizer. But the children do survive: "There are no verdicts to childhood, only consequences, and the bright freight of memory."

10. *Why Do I Love These People: Honest and Amazing Stories of Real Families* by Po Bronson. Remember the infamous cartoon of all the empty seats at the annual convention of adult children of normal parents? Most of the subjects of these essays get the joke. In these moving stories, they tell of their struggles not to create perfect families, just better ones, in the face of enormous hardship. There is bickering. Grudges are harbored. "There are problems galore!" says Bronson. "The test is not whether we have problems, but how we deal with them."

THAT DIG UP FAMILY ROOTS

1. *No Great Mischief* by Alistair MacLeod. "Living in the past is not living up to your potential." When Toronto dentist Alexander MacDonald spots that slogan on a T-shirt, he reacts with an appropriate sense of irony. For him, the past is prologue, and blood couldn't run any thicker. Even though he's the bookish brother who got away, he can't forget the red-haired clan that planted its flag on Cape Breton, or the debt owed to his older brother, Calum. Their disparate fortunes frame a poignant novel contrasting the limitations and benevolence of the ties that bind.

2. *The View From Castle Rock: Stories* by Alice Munro. A master of the short story, Munro has always plumbed her own life for material, but this collection of interlocked stories gets more autobiographical than any that came before. Tracing her roots back to a rugged Scottish valley and following it forward to the windswept Canadian plains, she paints the picture of a stoic clan that wrested a living from the land. "People I know say that work like this is restorative and has a peculiar dignity," she writes of the farm life she grew up with, "but I was born to it and feel it differently."

3. *The Namesake* by Jhumpa Lahiri. In this textured novel, ricocheting between Boston and Calcutta, Gogol Ganguli, an American-born child of Indian parents, rejects his namesake (the "pet name" given to him by his father at birth in honor of the

Russian writer) and adapts the more formal moniker, Nikhil (a Bengali name his family never used). It's the perfect metaphor for the pain of cultural assimilation. Rice Krispies or dal? People with split identities can neither completely reject nor completely embrace their ethnicity. For them, caught between two cultures, "There is no such thing as a perfect name."

4. *Beet Queen* by Louise Erdrich. In 1932, Abigail Adare's three children watch as she takes off into the sky with a barnstormer at a Minnesota carnival. Abandoned, the trio is soon separated: The baby is kidnapped; Karl rides the rails; Mary tracks down her aunt and cousin. But like the "complicated house" of a spider's web, the threads of their lives cross again. Spanning more than forty years and moving from Minneapolis to the beet fields and Indian reservations of North Dakota, this lyrical novel, told in multiple voices, is a testament to the fierce tenacity of family.

5. *The Cry of the Dove* by Fadia Faqir. In this novel, a Muslim woman named Salma tells of her struggle to adapt: After becoming pregnant out of wedlock, she barely escapes an honor killing by male members of her Bedouin tribe. Do-gooders spirit her out of harm's way, her newborn is returned to the tribe, and Salma emigrates to England to begin a new life. "They will kill you," her friend warns when she talks about returning to see the mother and daughter she misses so terribly. Faqir captures the hunger for home that defies reason but can't be ignored.

6. *Hanna's Daughters* by Marianne Fredriksson. Fredriksson's saga follows the lives of three generations of Swedish women:

Anna, a middle-aged writer; mother Johanna, who suffers from senile dementia; and grandmother Hanna, who once scoffed at her granddaughter's modern-day ambitions as too far-reaching for a girl. Exploring her matriarchal past after Hanna's death, Anna discovers her grandmother was right. A woman's life did await her, regardless of her dreams. All three women were shaped by their gender. "I didn't carry sacks of flour from the mill to the village, Grandmother. And yet I did."

7. *Middlesex* by Jeffrey Eugenides. A recessive gene and a "middlesex" child are the intriguing ingredients of this mind-blowing, five-hundred-plus page gender-bending family saga. The novel's narrator, a hermaphrodite, was raised in Detroit as a girl, but he really was a boy. He traces the genetic origins of this twist of fate back to 1920s Greece when his grandparents succumbed to incestuous love. A Greek tragedy? Not in America, where the fates aren't in charge. At fourteen, she/he underwent a sex operation and Calliope became Cal: "I was born twice; first, as a baby girl . . . and then again, as a teenage boy."

8. *Slaves in the Family* by Edward Ball. Of course, Ball has never owned slaves. His father never owned slaves. His father's father never owned slaves. But plenty in his family did, profiting from slave labor for 150 years. "The Balls lived side by side with black families for six generations," says Ball, who knew a lot about his early white ancestors but next to nothing about their many slaves. In this remarkable study, he pores over family documents, gathers oral histories, and traces his complete family history (not always a pretty picture), proudly adding black branches to his family tree.

9. *In My Blood: Six Generations of Madness and Desire in an American Family* by John Sedgwick. In his forties, novelist Sedgwick is depressed and suicidal. His problem, he realized, "wasn't the family *disease,* but the *family* disease, an excessive absorption of kinsmen"—meaning the Boston Brahmin types whose ambition and intensity left him a mixed legacy. An early ancestor "did not invent the social ladder. He merely climbed it." In the 1960s cousin Edie rode the wave as an Andy Warhol party girl until she overdosed on heroin. Sedgwick shows that privilege isn't always a lifesaving legacy.

10. *Finding Oprah's Roots, Finding Your Own* by Henry Louis Gates, Jr. Using detective work, history, and science, Harvard professor Gates traces Oprah Winfrey's family tree and makes a startling discovery: The television host is a fifth-generation entrepreneur. Does that mean ancestry is destiny? No, says Gates, but connecting the narrative of your family to a larger history can anchor you. This is especially true for African-Americans whose access to the past has been limited by slavery. "Genealogy can be a veritable time machine, enabling us all to be travelers through time and space."

FOR ADAPTING AND ADOPTING

1. *Love in the Driest Season* by Neely Tucker. Journalists are supposed to stay emotionally detached. But when foreign correspondent Tucker and his wife, Vita, an interracial couple from the American South on assignment in Africa, first see a tiny "girl-child" lying in a Zimbabwean orphanage, they drop all pretense of objectivity. In this achingly poignant mix of the personal and the political, Neely describes his wife's battle to nurse back to health this baby who had been abandoned at birth under an acacia tree, and their fight to adopt her. Why bother saving one out of millions in danger? Why not?

2. *The Women Who Raised Me* by Victoria Rowell. Here's a refreshing twist from the usual depressing memoir about foster care: In this case, the system worked. Several self-appointed moms stepped in to raise a little girl who had become a ward of the state because of her birth mother's mental illness. Rowell grew up to be a mom, an actress, and foster-care advocate: "Teachers, mentors, foster and adoptive parents, coaches, shelter providers, social workers, family members helping out . . . all caretakers deserve tribute from the person to whom they gave a hand."

3. *Two Little Girls: A Memoir of Adoption* by Theresa Reid. When Reid and her husband decided to go overseas to build their family, the red tape was almost a deal breaker, and his skills as a pediatrician led them to reject one child who appeared to have undiagnosed brain damage. But after a deal was sealed and they brought home their first child, Reid felt bonded to her immediately. Admitting that she's still sensitive about being an adoptive family, she has no doubts about her devotion to her two daughters, who both came from the former Soviet Union. "I am inside my own family, and I know; I have personal experience of our love."

4. *Raising Hope* by Katie Willard. When her mother dies in child-birth and her father takes off, twelve-year-old Hope is left in the care of the foulmouthed Ruth, her father's sister, and prim Sara Lynn, her father's former lover, in this novel that will have cobbled-together families cheering. The two women had been fierce rivals since high school, but with the help of Sara Lynn's mother, they set aside their differences to raise the girl. Surrogate "moms" everywhere can relate to Sara Lynn's cry: "My daughter. She's not. Of course she's not. But, oh, in my heart she is. My Hope."

5. *There Is No Me Without You: One Woman's Odyssey to Rescue Her Country's Children* by Melissa Fay Greene. After her husband and daughter died, an Ethiopian woman named Harege-woin Teferra slipped into a deep depression, until a Catholic priest called and asked her to care for a girl whose parents had died from AIDS. Four years later, as foster mother of twenty-four, Teferra was raising a candle for the 1 million AIDS orphans in her country. Greene, an accomplished writer, adopted two children herself while making Teferra the centerpiece of reporting on AIDS in Africa.

6. *Love Walked In: A Novel* by Marisa de los Santos. When Martin Grace, whose name "shares all but three letters with 'Cary Grant,'" walks into Cornelia Brown's Philadelphia café, the thirty-one-year-old film buff thinks she's found true love. But in this engaging first novel, she finds out that life is a lot messier than a romantic script, especially when "Cary Grant" comes with baggage: a commitment phobia, an unstable ex-wife, and an abandoned eleven-year-old daughter. Taking the latter under her wing, Brown embraces the real power of love: "Knowing what you love and why is as real as it gets."

7. *The Lost Daughters of China: Abandoned Girls, Their Journey to America, and the Search for a Missing Past* by Karin Evans. Tens of thousands of American households have joined a major cross-cultural story of our times by adopting girls from China. A one-child policy and male-minded family structure has made females so dispensable that 5 percent of the population is AWOL, Evans reports. This shocking statistic contrasts with the presence of Evans's two young daughters, Kelly and Franny, whose adoption seemed "as perfectly timed and inevitable as the ebb and flow of the tides."

8. *The Girls Who Went Away: The Hidden History of Women Who Surrendered Children for Adoption in the Decades Before* Roe v. Wade by Ann Fessler. This investigative work offers voice to the millions of young women who got pregnant outside marriage and gave up their babies in the decades after World War II. "You walked out of the hospital with whatever memories you had and the stretch marks on your body," one mother remembers. Shame and helplessness silenced the anguish, but for many the sense of loss has stayed with them throughout their lives.

9. *The Good Mother* by Sue Miller. When Anna Dunlap splits with her lawyer husband, she takes custody of three-year-old Molly while her ex moves to D.C. with his new bride. Anna finds work to pay the bills and a new boyfriend to share their life in Cambridge, but the risks in their arrangement don't register until

it's too late. Earth to Anna: Sleepovers may be okay for grown-ups, but they aren't so good when kids are involved. She is stunned to lose her daughter in a custody fight, as novelist Miller explores contemporary sexual mores and the complications created by broken families.

10. *The Mistress's Daughter* by A. M. Homes. Read this memoir less for the gritty details than to observe the author's rage at her biological parents. Novelist Homes was adopted as an infant and knew little of her birth parents until she was an adult. Then her birth mom made contact. Oddly, Homes rebuffed her but went searching for her birth dad, who was alternately charming and distant even after a DNA test proved his paternity. Describing their tangled relationship, Homes shows how she unconsciously repeated the pattern set by her mother and gives you insight into the hurt that helped provoke her dark fiction.

ABOUT RAISING KIDS
(NOT THE FAIRY-TALE VERSION)

1. *Wiped: Life With a Pint-Sized Dictator* by Rebecca Eckler. Bridget Jones in diapers: This is definitely not your genteel mom's guide to dealing with a newborn. But Canadian journalist Eckler, author of *Knocked Up: Confessions of a Hip Mother-to-be*, helps new mothers laugh through their tears with the Mommy moments people forget to tell you: (1) You will feel like a walk-

ing, talking zombie; (2) you will obsess about the pregnancy pounds that haven't gone away; and (3) newborns can be very, very boring.

2. *Great With Child* by Beth Ann Fennelly. "I rarely write real, old-fashioned letters anymore; hardly anyone does," Fennelly begins. Here, the poet and mother makes an exception, sending regular missives to a former student, who is pregnant. They are alternately moving, funny, and practical, with an unusual honesty about just how hard it is to be a young mother. Favorite line: "What I want to say today, sweet friend, is no matter how busy you become as the mother of a newborn, make sure you read in a good book every day, even if it's just for a few minutes."

3. *The Early Birds: A Mother's Story for Our Times* by Jenny Minton. Having babies can be as easy as falling off a log—or not. For Minton, it takes fertility treatments to become pregnant, and then she gives birth two months early to twin boys. As she describes her harrowing experience as the mother of preemies, she notes her willingness to "erase myself if it will help Sam and Gus to thrive." She also points out that fertility drugs have lifted the number of multiple births, pushing up the infant mortality rate. And yet, this is no cautionary tale; it's a story about gratitude.

4. *The Making of a Mother: Overcoming the Nine Key Challenges, From Crib to Empty Nest* by Valerie Davis Raskin. A clinical psychiatrist who specializes in motherhood sums up the job in a big-picture way that includes the need to set limits, make room for your partner, accept the imperfection of schools and other

institutions that serve your child, and revise dreams to accord with whom your child is becoming. "The duty of a mother is to help her child not need her," she points out. Her college-bound son puts this a different way: "Mom, you've had eighteen years to teach me values. Chill."

5. *Get Out of My Life, but First Could You Drive Me & Cheryl to the Mall: A Parent's Guide to the New Teenager* by Anthony E. Wolf. Teenagers are "mouthier, less directly obedient, especially at home" than in less permissive times, but teen rebellion has always been a necessary stage, says clinical psychologist Wolf. Distinguishing between what teens say and how they feel, he explains why girls pick fights and boys tune out and why good parenting sometimes involves letting go. The good news? "The unabated nastiness does run its course and fade away."

6. *Perfect Madness: Motherhood in the Age of Anxiety* by Judith Warner. Warner steps back to look at how motherhood fits within the confines of American culture, and her conclusions aren't pretty. In this country, moms assume responsibility with few of the extended support systems found elsewhere. Work pressures often add to their load. "And because they can't, humanly, take everything onto themselves, they simply go nuts." Don't fight for perfection or with each other, Warner advises. If you fight for anything, it should be family-friendly public policy.

7. *Amy and Isabelle* by Elizabeth Strout. Keeping tabs on a wayward teen is especially tough for a single parent, who only has one set of eyes and ears. In this novel about a mother trying to protect her child from harm, a daughter's sexual awakening sounds a very loud alarm for Isabelle Goodrow, who paid dearly for her own mistakes at that age. Alas, never underestimate the power of a sixteen-year-old to get under the radar. Amy seems set on a path of destruction, if only to demonstrate the truth, that she and her mom are "sick and exhausted with their stupid lives."

8. *Reviving Ophelia: Saving the Selves of Adolescent Girls* by Mary Pipher and Ruth Ross. Long before Britney Spears came on the scene, therapist Pipher quantified the dangers facing teen girls. In this classic, she describes the "social and developmental Bermuda Triangle" created by their hormones and our highly sexualized and media-saturated culture. But beyond the jeremiad, Pipher explains how the typical adolescent girl thinks—in extremes and generalities—and offers practical ways to show them how to separate thinking from feeling, validate themselves, and care about others.

9. *The Good Son: Shaping the Moral Development of Our Boys and Young Men* by Michael Gurian. Granted, men have the upper hand in society, says Gurian, a therapist who has made boys his specialty. But don't confuse that with the challenges they face as boys. With brains designed for a task at a time—for example, kill or be killed—they are "morally fragile," he says. What's more, while girls are biologically programmed for motherhood, boys do not have such an inherent and obvious path to self-worth. This book is a thoughtful guide for keeping them on track.

10. *Before and After: A Novel* by Rosellen Brown. How far would you go to defend your teen in trouble? This is the agonizing question raised when Jacob Reiser, the seventeen-year-old son of a middle-class Jewish family in a rural New England town, is accused of killing his girlfriend. Not everyone in the Reiser family agrees on an answer, but in the end the dad's agony is clear. "What it comes down to is, the worse our history the more we had to stay together—only we knew all the parts, good and bad, even if we added them up differently."

THAT SHOW MOTHERHOOD IS FOREVER (AND FATHERHOOD, TOO)

1. *Walking on Eggshells: Navigating the Delicate Relationship Between Adult Children and Parents* by Jane Isay. As the mother of two grown sons, former book editor Isay notes that her generation was the first to raise kids permissively. Now they're being trained to "enjoy living on the periphery of their children's lives." But not many parents—including Isay—dig the sideline role. Concerted effort, self-control, and clarity are essential, she observes somewhat ruefully. She concludes that parents and their children are saved by the force field that irrevocably draws them to one another: "You can smash a family, but the basic energy will pull it back together."

2. *Broken: My Story of Addiction and Redemption* by William Cope Moyers and Katherine Ketcham. The pivotal moment in

this story about being a privileged son and blowing it repeatedly comes when Moyers, the son of famous TV journalist Bill Moyers, has yet another relapse. Arriving to pick him up at a crack house, the elder Moyers tells him, "I'm finished." By this time his son is thirty-five, with a family of his own, and there seemed little wisdom in Daddy rescuing him. Given all his second chances, the younger Moyers is right to deliver his story of addiction and recovery with humility. "I'm done, God," he finally says. "Have me."

3. *The Shell Seekers* by Rosamunde Pilcher. Children don't always cherish what you do, Pilcher's novel warns. Penelope Keeling learns this when her two grown children push her to sell *The Shell Seekers,* a beloved painting by her father that now has risen in value. They insist it's for her sake, but she knows better. "What had become of the babies she had borne and loved," she asks of her money-grubbing offspring. "The answer was, perhaps, that she had not expected enough of them."

4. *Unless* by Carol Shields. Forty-four-year-old writer Reta Winters is bereft because her nineteen-year-old daughter, Norah, has dropped out of college and sits on a Toronto street corner wearing a sign that says, "Goodness." Her child's retreat from a callous world puts Reta in a state of panic and guilt about the child she raised to believe in herself—only to learn, as she laments, that "women are excluded from greatness." Reta's own willingness to settle for small accomplishments offers ironic contrast in this novel, Shields's last, which finds the truth in the saying that a mother is only as happy as her unhappiest child.

5. *We're Still Family: What Grown Children Have to Say About Their Parents' Divorce* by Constance Ahrons. Divorce doesn't destroy families—it rearranges them, says sociologist (and divorced mother) Ahrons: "Families *can* and *do* adapt and thrive in the face of change." Her advice in this guide to divorced parents and their children: Give up your nucléar family bias and accept these new untidy family ties. If you get over your divorce, so will your children. "Even though they don't fit the Norman Rockwell image, to the people living in them these messy extended tribes are family."

6. *Black & White* by Dani Shapiro. The idea that a mom should sacrifice for her kids is so ingrained that it comes as a shock when she exploits them, instead. In this novel, the art photographer Ruth Dunne climbed to fame—and notoriety—with nude and suggestive pictures of her pubescent daughter, Clara. At eighteen, Clara cut off all contact, but when her mother is dying from cancer fourteen years later, she returns home. The deathbed reunion is not pretty. Sadly, sometimes ruptures are so severe that someone else has to say the magic words: "She wanted to do right by you, my dear."

7. *Alexander and the Wonderful, Marvelous, Excellent, Terrific Ninety Days: An Almost Completely Honest Account of What Happened to Our Family When Our Youngest Came to Live with Us for Three Months* by Judith Viorst. When her son (who inspired Viorst's children's book about that boy who had a "no good, very bad day") moves back home with his wife and three kids (temporarily, due to house renovations), the comic writer tries her best to enjoy the chaotic invasion. As this wry account demonstrates, she mostly succeeds: "When you give you ought to give with both hands."

8. *Trespass* by Valerie Martin. "She gave you a hat. I gave you your life." That's Chloe Dale's remark after her twenty-year-old son, Toby, brings home his exotic new love, Salome. Chloe worries because she's a Croatian refugee, but the truth is that Chloe herself is the mother-in-law from hell, incensed over losing her boy. Meanwhile, the temperamental Salome explores the secret of her own lost mother in a novel where the voice of reason is male: "It doesn't matter what either of us thinks," Chloe's husband tells her. "You're just going to have to make the best of it." Words to live by!

9. *Paula* by Isabel Allende. "Listen, Paula, I am going to tell you a story," begins the author of *The House of Spirits* in this touching memoir. She is speaking to her twenty-eight-year-old comatose daughter. She tells tales of ancestral spirits and her native Chile, even when she knows Paula will never wake up. How can she stop? In a letter she asked to have opened only after she died which was eerily written a year before she fell ill, Paula echoes her mother's faith in enduring bonds: "Don't be sad. We will be together as long as you remember me."

10. *I Only Say This Because I Love You: Talking to Your Parents, Partner, Sibs, and Kids When You're All Adults* by Deborah Tannen. Thinking about joining the Biting Tongue Club when dealing

with your adult children or elderly parents? Try instead to understand how talk works in families, says linguist Tannen in this absorbing look at the many minefields relatives traverse in their conversations. Watch out for subtext, intended or not. What is said (the message) is not always what is heard (the metamessage), she warns. "Talk in the family is an ongoing balancing act."

FOR WHEN ONLY A GIRLFRIEND WILL DO

1. *Girls' Night Out: Celebrating Women's Groups Across America* by Tamara Kreinin and Barbara Camens. In a combination of pictures and text, this showcase of women's groups across the country includes a motorcycle brigade, the "Bridgies" (bridge players), and a mother-daughter book club created to give teenagers and their moms "a safe place to talk." Encouraging women to join forces in self-created clubs, the authors note that the activity matters less than the chance to empower each other, keep friendships alive and share responsibility for the more needy members of the tribe.

2. *The Faith Club: A Muslim, A Christian, A Jew—Three Women Search for Understanding* by Ranya Idliby, Suzanne Oliver, and Priscilla Warner. After 9/11, three mothers—all of different faiths—felt empowered to meet on a regular basis to talk about being Muslim, Christian, and Jewish. Here, you can eavesdrop on their freewheeling, no-holds-barred conversations about such sticky topics as who killed Jesus, what is jihad, and religious stereotyping. You hear them laughing, arguing, challenging each other, and becoming friends. Intrigued? They even provide a guide to starting your own Faith Club.

3. *The Red Tent* by Anita Diamant. Speaking of women and religion, Diamant fleshes out female characters from the Hebrew Bible with such realism that you'll swear she's uncovered some lost scrolls. Dinah, daughter of Leah and Jacob, only gets a passing mention in the Book of Genesis, but here she and other biblical women come to life. Imagine listening "in the ruddy shade of the red tent, the menstrual tent" to these timeless stories of birthing and weaning, cooking and spinning, but also of betrayal, rape, and revenge, tales still passed on woman to woman.

4. *All Is Vanity* by Christina Schwarz. To end her writer's block while struggling on a novel, Margaret shamelessly seizes on the woes of lifelong friend Letty as source material in this wickedly funny satire. Letty, bogged down with three children, an ambitious husband, and the pressures of consumer-crazy L.A., sends increasingly desperate (and side-splitting) e-mails to her friend about her overspending. Margaret eggs her on with an eye to a juicier story. Alas, Letty should have been more suspicious. Admits Margaret: "Even in our games, she was always Robin to my Batman."

5. *Catfight: Rivalries Among Women—From Diets to Dating* by Leora Tanenbaum. Here's a sad-but-true commentary on female friendship, showing how camaraderie and even healthy competition can turn sour. Why does this happen? According to Tanenbaum, because the world still puts more value on a man's opinion. So women are easily tempted to set aside solidarity to impress a guy or win a race (first place beats Miss Congeniality). Tanenbaum says it's a divide-and-conquer strategy that women should recognize but not abide. "We must not be consoled with the bread crumbs of petty power."

6. *Snow Flower and the Secret Fan* by Lisa See. See's novel about female friendship in nineteenth-century China is based on a real custom of pairing young girls to be lifelong companions ("old sames"). In old age, Lily, the narrator, looks back without questioning the oppressive traditions imposed on her. But why should she? Her husband's worldly success served her well. Not so for her alter ego, Snow Flower, yet Lily doesn't forsake her. "She was the only one ever who saw my weaknesses and loved me in spite of them. And I had loved her even when I hated her most."

7. *A Thousand Splendid Suns* by Khaled Hosseini. Sharing the same husband doesn't sound like a road to collegiality between two women. But in the case of Mariam and Laila, the Afghani wives of a man neither wanted to marry, his cruelties forge a bond so strong that no sacrifice is too great. Through their lives you see a society with so little regard for women that wife beating is commonplace and childbirth without anesthetics is standard practice. This second novel from the author of *The Kite Runner* is a searing indictment of how women were treated under Taliban rule.

8. *The Knitting Circle* by Ann Hood. This comfort food of a novel about the power of friendship to heal is based on the death of the author's child. The fictional Mary Baxter is coaxed into a group of women who knit together soon after she loses her five-year-old daughter, Stella. In the quiet company of the group, she hopes to escape the trauma of death and illness. Instead, Mary finds out that some of the other women also have heavy burdens. Gradually, she learns that, while there's no escape from sorrow, an open heart increases the capacity for joy.

9. *Truth and Beauty: A Friendship* by Ann Patchett. In graduate school, Patchett launched a twenty-year friendship with fellow writer Lucy Grealy, whose face was deformed by cancer that destroyed part of her jaw. As told in this honest but loving tribute, she was a wounded bird who compensated for a lifetime of surgeries by acting out with sex and drugs, as well as a manipulator who trusted her beloved "Anngora" to act as the grown-up. Patchett's warnings failed to prevent Grealy's death from an accidental heroin overdose in 2002, a loss she still mourns: "Even when Lucy was devastated or difficult, she was the person I knew best in the world, the person I was the most comfortable with."

10. *On Beauty* by Zadie Smith. Smith's sprawling comic novel is about race, academic (and artistic) pretensions, adolescent longings, and an unlikely friendship between two women. Kiki, an oversized, exuberant black Floridian, is married to the WASPy Howard. The frail Carlene is wed to the Trinidadian Sir Monty. Both husbands are art scholars and rivals. When Carlene bequeaths Kiki an expensive painting in her will (a purposeful nod to E. M. Forster's *Howards End*, whose structure Smith has echoed), the tender connection between the two wives reminds everyone: Love and beauty are best when you least expect them.

THAT SAY PETS ARE PEOPLE, TOO

1. *Marley and Me: Life and Love With the World's Worst Dog* by John Grogan. With books about dogs always flooding the market, what has made *Marley* so special? Sure, newspaper columnist Grogan has a way with words (though he never had his way with the wild-eyed Marley), but this story of his family's unqualified love of a drooling, exasperating, and overexuberant Lab also speaks to a seldom-admitted but comforting truth: Less-than-perfect children are the source of parents' best stories. "A person can learn a lot from a dog, even a loopy one like ours."

2. *Shaggy Muses: The Dogs Who Inspired Virginia Woolf, Emily Dickinson, Elizabeth Barrett Browning, Edith Wharton, and Emily Brontë* by Maureen Adams. Pinka, Carlo, Flush, Mitou, and Keeper may not be as famous as their owners, but they have their own literary pedigree, says psychologist Adams. Think you know these writers? Picture a reclusive Dickinson out for long walks with a lumbering Newfoundland. Or Browning coming out of her depression, thanks to a lapdog. And who would have thought that the refined Wharton could be so sentimental: "My little dog / A heart-beat / At my feet."

3. *Dogs That Know When Their Owners Are Coming Home: And Other Unexplained Powers of Animals* by Rupert Sheldrake. Pets and extrasensory perception may seem an unlikely combination, but only if you haven't spent much time with a four-footed companion. Sheldrake combines evolutionary biology with recent research and his own speculation to contend that animals are telepathic, have an inexplicable sense of direction, and sense events before they happen. Skeptics, be advised: Sheldrake holds a doctorate in biochemistry from Cambridge.

4. *I Am the Cat, Don't Forget That: Feline Expressions* by Valerie Shaff and Roy Blount Jr. "Dogs, clearly, wish they could talk. . . . A cat tunes in on a need-to-know basis," says funnyman Blount, who pairs up with photographer Shaff for this book of ditties that explores what's behind those various feline expressions. A wide-eyed tabby expounds: "I can tell what you are thinking— / You think / I don't blink. / Maybe I blink while you are blinking." Another, on his back, lazily reminds you: "When I purr / Don't infer / it's because you pat. / No, you pat / because I purr / I am the cat / Don't forget that."

5. *Animals in Translation: Using the Mysteries of Autism to Decode Animal Behavior* by Temple Grandin and Catherine Johnson. You may think you wouldn't care about what it takes cattle to go through a narrow chute. But Grandin, an animal-behavior expert, will convince you otherwise in this absorbing book about

learning to think like other mammals—which means obsessively, one thing at a time, and often relying on the nose, which humans barely employ. Grandin, whose autism helped her become a professional "animal whisperer," shows how sentient these critters are.

6. *Riding Lessons* by Sara Gruen. The author of the best seller *Water for Elephants* keeps showing her love for animals. In this novel, an accident during a competition ends the Olympic dreams of young Annemarie Zimmer. She settles for a routine job and humdrum life until she hits a trifecta: She gets fired, loses her husband to another woman, and discovers that their teenager is off the rails, all on the same day. With daughter in clutches, she returns to the family home and the stables that once were her life. There she reclaims the feisty spirit that suggests Annemarie will, in truth and spirit, get back on her horse.

7. *Dog* by Michelle Herman. Middle-aged and childless, the fictional Jill Rosen (she prefers to be called J.T.) is teaching at a New York college (her poetry career had fizzled) when she adopts a puppy featured on a dog-rescue website. The dog turns her life upside down, "not necessarily a bad thing." This is a tender story about aging and loneliness, about how you need to trust your own crazy feelings, and about how dogs can teach you to feel again: "He was a dog. Why did she have to remind herself of this so often?"

8. *Cat People: A Hilariously Entertaining Look at the World of Cat Lovers and Their Obsessive Devotion to Their Pets* by Margaret and Michael Korda. Publishing pooh-bah Michael Korda

came late to his infatuation with cats, but now he is just as smitten as his wife, Margaret. Together they lovingly describe the cats
in their lives, many of whom adopted them on their Hudson
River Valley farm. Their book on all things cats is chockablock
with cat facts, from the reasons people don't like felines to
Churchill's devotion to (and conversations with) his cat, Nelson.

9. *A Three Dog Life* by Abigail Thomas. After a hit-and-run accident that leaves her husband's memory shattered, Abigail's
friends urge her to ditch the beagle that Rich chased into traffic.
But it is that dog who helps her through the trauma of dealing
with a spouse who lives in an eternal present. She doesn't desert
Rich, either. Committing him to an institution, she buys a home
nearby and adopts two more dogs. In this deeply affecting memoir, she describes her three-dog life, where everything changes
except her husband: "He never knows I'm leaving until I go."

10. *The Good Good Pig: The Extraordinary Life of Christopher
Hogwood* by Sy Montgomery. From a runty piglet small enough
to fit into a shoe box, Montgomery's good, good pig grew to over
750 pounds. In this heartfelt account of her life with the doughnut-
loving Christopher Hogwood (named after the conductor), the
naturalist talks of pig slops, pig diets, and how this "Big Buddha
master" brought together a Yankee community (and helped her
deal with a difficult mother). Chris died peacefully in his sleep at
fourteen, adored and pampered to the end.

LOVE, SEX, &
SECOND CHANCES

Love, especially romantic love, is not an easy concept to pin down.

Medieval troubadours sang its praises. Bob Dylan sings, "Love Is a Four-Letter Word." In Erich Segal's best seller *Love Story*, a man and a dying woman discover that love means never having to say you're sorry. In Dante's *Inferno*, Francesca and Paolo are a sorry pair, condemned forever to the second circle of hell for falling in love. Their adulterous affair was sparked by reading about Lancelot and Guinevere, another couple doomed by passion.

"What do any of us really know about love?" asks Mel McGinnis in Raymond Carver's short story "What We Talk About When We Talk About Love." "It seems to me we're just beginners at love. . . . You know the kind of love I'm talking about now. Physical love, that impulse that drives you to someone special, as well as love of the other person's being, his or her essence, as it were. Carnal love and, well, call it sentimental love, the day to day caring about the other person."

The books in this section struggle with romantic love in all its permutations: love found, love lost, sex without love, love without sex. They celebrate enduring bonds but are keenly aware of the difficulties that go with achieving them. They confront the bitterness and heartache that love can bring but also are open to finding it in the most unexpected places. They offer advice on keeping relationships hot and learning how to recalculate when things go wrong. They peer into the psyche of the opposite sex.

As society's views of women's roles and women's sense of themselves have changed, romantic liaisons have become more complicated and more intriguing. As women vacillate between the desire for independence and the need for intimacy, relationships are sometimes strained. Women want the right to be heard, but, like the leading ladies swooning in Victorian novels, they're still partial to wine and roses.

Those swooning ladies—beautiful, emotional, and passive— first appeared at the end of the eighteenth century in Jean Jacques Rousseau's *Emile* and other novels by proponents of the Romantic Movement. Those romantic heroines were a male invention, and by the nineteenth century, the conventions of their stories were set: Woman meets True Love. Woman fights the objections of class, family, and/or social mores. Woman unites with True Love and lives happily ever after.

Even women writers embraced the concept—although the best of them toned down the passive part. But in the novels of Jane Austen and the Brontës, the female protagonists were aggressive for love, not self-actualization. Jane Eyre ends up winning Edward Rochester. His unruly first wife, the madwoman in the attic, only later became a symbol of feminist anger and revolt. When Becky Sharp attempts to act on her own in William Makepeace Thackeray's *Vanity Fair,* she is not seen as a positive role model but as an uppity female. In the traditional world of the romantic heroine, a woman was defined by the man she managed to land.

When the modern romance novel first appeared in the early '70s, it was packaged in paperback and embraced the basic elements of that original heroine: a meek woman overpowered by an alpha male. Consider this scene from Kathleen Woodiwiss's 1972 *The Flame and the Flower,* credited with being the first modern romance tale:

"Her ivory skin glowed softly in the candlelight. . . . He moved closer and in a rapid movement slipped his arm about her narrow waist, nearly lifting her from the floor, and then covered her mouth with his, engulfing Heather in a heady scent, not unlike that of a brandy her father had been fond of. She was too surprised to resist and hung limp in his embrace."

But this kind of a scene was a throwback: Contemporary romance novels soon began to reflect women's evolving attitudes about their right to be heard. Rape scenes disappeared. Savvier about the world than the Heathers of the genre, the new romantic heroine grapples with modern themes, from single parenting to domestic abuse. She no longer is obliged to be weak and helpless, but often is an older working woman seeking an equal relationship with a man. She isn't always a virgin, and she's not always ivory skinned. Romance lines also now feature black, Latino, and Asian heroines. There are chaste romances aimed at Christian readers. By 2000, even the covers changed, as heaving breasts gave way to bucolic landscapes.

Meanwhile, beyond the romance genre, the presumptions have also changed. Happy endings are not unheard of, but happiness has been reexamined and redefined. A woman doesn't always end up with a man to find her life satisfying. Sometimes she ends up with a she. Sometimes she is happy just being on her own.

In Carver's short story, the four characters seated around a kitchen table polishing off bottles of gin—McGinnis, his wife, Terri, and their friends Nick and Laura—touch on all kinds of love: erotic, passionate, and long-lasting, but also fleeting, codependent, and even violent. McGinnis, who is a cardiologist, dominates the conversation, but as the light dims and they continue to argue about just what love is, you realize: Even a heart specialist cannot explain its elusive nature.

ABOUT ENDURING BONDS

1. *Married: A Fine Predicament* by Anne Roiphe. "It is not good to go through life alone," begins this defense of wedded bliss from a twice-married writer and mother of grown daughters. Sure, divorce has its place, Roiphe writes, but she wouldn't wish the pain on anybody. With a feminist's voice and a sentimental heart, she strolls through the litany of issues marriage creates but casts her vote for fidelity and togetherness. Don't believe everyone who says their spouse is to blame, she says: "Some people who think they are in unhappy marriages are just in unhappy bodies."

2. *The Stone Carvers* by Jane Urquhart. In a novel that says love lost is seldom forgotten, Canadian villager Karla Becker learns the art of woodcarving from her grandfather as a girl. But she abandons the skill after her lover, Eamon, fails to return from the "reverse migration" that filled the trenches of Europe during World War I. "This was the way it was going to be then," she realizes bitterly, his absence always "controlling the colour of her days." But the construction of a monument to the missing gives Karla consolation and a reason to return to her craft. The alchemy of hope permeates this story.

3. *Crossing to Safety* by Wallace Stegner. The landscape of marriage is largely hidden from view, mysterious not only to outsiders but also to the participants themselves. In this semiautobiographical novel about two couples and their lifelong friendship, Stegner quietly charts the flow of marriage from the perspective of Larry Morgan, our nominee for most humane male narrator in contemporary fiction. Whether he's kissing his wife's pregnant belly ("solid as wood," he notes) or confronting old age ("Can I survive her?"), Larry shows the meaning and beauty in "until death do us part."

4. *The Long Embrace: Raymond Chandler and the Woman He Loved* by Judith Freeman. The iconic mystery writer made no mystery of how he felt about his wife, Cissy. Nearly two decades older than he, she was more "mamma mia!" than a mom substitute. As Freeman treks around Los Angeles exploring Chandler's life and haunts, Cissy figures as the mystery man's muse and model for his fictional hotties. "You can make all sorts of jokes about sex, mostly lewd," he wrote, "but at the bottom of his heart every decent man feels that his approach to the woman he loves is an approach to a shrine."

5. *The Best Day the Worst Day: Life With Jane Kenyon* by Donald Hall. Poet Hall begins this memoir with Kenyon's death, at forty-seven, of leukemia. But he quickly turns back to their twenty-three-year marriage, a May–December union that began when she was his student at the University of Michigan. He recalls their time writing poetry and braving tough winters in a "rapture of quiet" on his family's New Hampshire farm. He remembers their shared fight against Kenyon's cancer and her much longer struggle with depression. Both had planned for the older Hall to die first. A decade after her death, Hall writes, "Jane fills the air around me like a rainy day."

6. *This Old Spouse: A Do-It-Yourself Guide to Restoring, Renovating, and Rebuilding Your Relationship* by Sharyn Wolf. Marriages are a lot like houses, says Wolf, who puts that metaphor to good use in her therapy practice. The language of home repair is both a whimsical and useful way of addressing marital woes: Does your wiring (communication skills) need upgrading? Is your plumbing (sex life) clogged? Here, she teaches you how to be your own contractor, overseeing the major and minor repairs every marriage eventually needs. Remember: "When it comes to marriage, they're all fixer-uppers."

7. *The Time Traveler's Wife* by Audrey Niffenegger. Henry is a man suffering from "chrono-impairment," a disorder that causes him to travel through time and space at a moment's notice. Clare is his wife, who serves as his anchor between these disruptions. Alternating between their two voices, first-time novelist Niffenegger makes you utterly believe this wild, intriguing plot. As she pitches Henry into the future and back to the past with dazzling ease, she provides an entertaining and strangely moving symbol for the permanence of human connections. As Henry tells Clare, when it comes to love, "time is nothing."

8. *The Woman Who Waited: A Novel* by Andrei Makine. The narrator of this lyrical novel is an unnamed twenty-six-year-old researcher documenting the customs of a Russian village emptied of its able-bodied sons during World War II. Now, thirty years later, a handful of old women remain, along with a forty-something woman named Vera. Vera, who was sixteen when her fiancé left for war, is said to be still waiting for his return. Obsessed with this romantic story, the young researcher pursues Vera, but questions his motives: Is he in love with a woman or merely the idea that love could ever be so faithful?

9. *The History of Love* by Nicole Krauss. This touching novel features two unforgettable characters: Alma Singer, a teen coping with her father's death, and Leo Gursky, a wry octogenarian afraid of dying alone. Both are linked to *The History of Love* written by Gursky before World War II. The manuscript, which Gursky thought lost, was published under another man's name and inspired Alma's parents to name their daughter after the woman the book immortalizes. But loss—of books or people—isn't what makes soul mates of this unlikely pair; it's their mutual belief in love's constancy that draws them together.

10. *Twenty Love Poems and a Song of Despair* by Pablo Neruda. Nobel Prize–winning poet Neruda didn't idealize love but linked it to the sounds and smells of nature and ordinary lives, says author Cristina Garcia in her introduction to this collection. His twenty-one poems, odes to love lost and love found, "encourage me to look closely at my own world for small miracles and the persistence of love," she says. Even Neruda's songs of despair (and there are more than one here) speak to love's enduring power: "Love is so short, forgetting is so long."

ABOUT ROMANCE
WHEN YOU LEAST EXPECT IT

1. *My Dream of You* by Nuala O'Faolain. On the eve of her fiftieth birthday, Kathleen, a writer living alone in a basement apartment in London, has all but given up on love in this novel about second chances. Seeking to dispel her cynicism, she returns to her native Ireland to research a 150-year-old tale of an infamous love affair between a rich English woman and her Irish groomsman during the time of the Irish famine. Did this woman really defy class and culture for love? In this story within a story, Kathleen uncovers a more complicated truth—and finds her own unexpected path to love in the process.

2. *Tolstoy Lied: A Love Story* by Rachel Kadish. Marriage, who needs it? That's the conclusion of Tracy Farber, English professor and feminist, who at thirty-three is the expert on everybody else's love life but has given up on her own. Until, of course, she meets a banjo-playing Canadian named George. ("I'm Jewish," she announces on their first date, trying to put some distance between them. He calls her bluff, replying, "I didn't invite you out to talk you into a personal relationship with your savior.") Kadish cleverly twists a chick-lit plot into a novel that contrasts how love works in theory with the real deal. It's seldom tidy.

3. *Dona Flor and Her Two Husbands: A Moral and Amorous Tale* by Jorge Amado. After Dona Flor's charming but no-good husband drops dead during Brazil's carnival, she remarries his polar opposite—a dull pharmacist who offers fidelity and a steady income. Alas, when she can't stop thinking of first hubby's hot kisses, who would have thought her longing would conjure his ghost, lusty as ever, ready to join her in a ménage à trois? But Amado's bawdy novel, written forty years ago, underlines a universal, timeless truth: Women long for both security and passion but rarely get both.

4. *The Price of Salt* by Patricia Highsmith. Think Thelma and Louise as lovers minus the car-crash ending. That's the plot of this 1952 novel, daring in its day and thought to have inspired Nabokov's *Lolita*. Therese Belivet, an aspiring stage designer, meets Carol Aird, a married woman, while selling toys in a department store. Soon they're obsessed with each other, and then they're on the road. But real escape is futile: A detective in hot pursuit will determine the fate of their relationship. More fascinating than their same-sex romance is the power balance between them.

5. *The Abstinence Teacher* by Tom Perrotta. High school sex-ed teacher Ruth Ramsey is a single mother determined to raise her daughter with her own liberal views. Tim Mason is her daughter's soccer coach, a former druggie who has found religion and gladly bears witness with his players. You can guess where the tension lies—in a mutual attraction that has to rise above the twosome's differing values. Perrotta takes aim at the hypocrisy of the religious right, but the important part of the story is about two injured souls struggling to find themselves—and, maybe, each other.

6. *Dared and Done: The Marriage of Elizabeth Barrett and Robert Browning* by Julia Markus. How do I love thee? In spite of Daddy, it turns out. When her father wouldn't allow his children to marry, Elizabeth became a morphine-addicted invalid whose poetry lured an admirer, Robert, to her London home. At age thirty-nine, she "chose life over death," and they eloped. At forty-three, she bore a baby boy. As Markus points out, the story of this famous love match is less the "happily ever after" of their poetry than the real-life union of a nurturing man and his genius wife.

7. *The Fortune Hunters: Dazzling Women and the Men They Married* by Charlotte Hays. "A fortune hunter is a woman who can never have a headache," notes this former gossip columnist, who says marrying a rich man is not the free ride you might expect. Her fresh appraisal of women with an eye for thick wallets includes, among others, Jackie O., Princess Di, Carolyn Bessette Kennedy, and gals who ended up as Mrs. Bass and Mrs. Vanderbilt. Hays deconstructs what it takes to be a successful schemer and delivers a surprise: Sometimes love and money *do* coincide.

8. *The White Masai* by Corinne Hofmann. Swiss businesswoman Hofmann bagged more than she bargained for on her Kenyan safari: She fell in love with a Masai warrior (he was wearing only a loincloth and jewelry), married him, had his child, and lived with him (and his mother) in his cow-dung hut. Amazingly, the marriage lasted four years, broken up by that most mundane of problems: a husband's jealousy. Sound like a wild fictional plot? This is a true story. Hofmann tells it with grace and feeling, making this improbable love seem inevitable: "I feel myself at one with this man."

9. *Brokeback Mountain* by Annie Proulx. The Western setting, albeit evocative, is the usual lodgepole pines, high meadows, dark mountains. But the love between Ennis and Jack comes as a surprise, even to themselves, in this heartbreaking short story. Herding sheep above the treeline on Brokeback Mountain, they are able to express what is forbidden below. For the next twenty years, their furtive affair survives everything but intolerance. Then only memories remain: "The intensely familiar odor of cigarettes, musky sweat, and a faint sweetness like grass, and with it the rushing cold of the mountain."

10. *Love in the Time of Cholera* by Gabriel Garcia Marquez. Boy meets girl. Girl rejects boy. Boy waits fifty years to get his chance again. Marquez's classic novel begins with a comical death (Fermina Daza's husband falls out of a mango tree while chasing a parrot) and ends with the long-delayed union of Daza and her old sweetheart, Florentino Ariza. The two chapters point to the unexpected twists life offers. But they also bookmark a tale that unexpectedly contains something rare in literature: sensual scenes of late-in-life romance. "It is life more than death that has no limits."

ABOUT ADULTERY, BETRAYAL, & MOVING ON

1. *Five Men Who Broke My Heart* by Susan Shapiro. Worried you married the wrong guy? In this hilarious and brutally honest memoir, writer Shapiro shares her perfect cure for such doubts: Look up your exes. She revisited the five men who broke her heart: Brad, George, and Tom, with alarming symmetry in July, August, and September ("single, married, divorcing"); gourmet Richard over lunch; and first love David over the Internet. Shapiro discovered the heartbreak inflicted was not so one-sided. Yes, she saw why she had been smitten by them, but also, as she told her husband, "why I married you."

2. *Poison* by Susan Fromberg Schaeffer. Any man who inspires two wives to put their heads in the oven brings to mind the late poet Ted Hughes, whose legacy is bogged down by these sui-cides. The pivotal figure in this novel, Peter Grosvenor, is a stand-in—although stand-in is not exactly right, as he's mostly six feet under in this fictional postmortem about a writer who juggled his work with a talent for making women miserable. Schaeffer imagines his lovers' contentious moves as he circles above the fray, an eagle who can see too late that "we are paid back for our arrogance."

3. *To Hell With Love: Poems to Mend a Broken Heart* by Mary D. Esselman and Elizabeth Ash Velez. Plotting sweet revenge? Indulging in melodramatic reconciliation fantasies? You need "literary therapy for the broken-hearted." This collection of poems, packaged in a volume that looks like a small prayer book, addresses all the emotions of a wrenching breakup: rage, sadness, self-hatred, false hope, relapse. But don't worry, the authors won't leave you drowning in self-pity. They also include verses for when you're ready to move on. Spain's Miguel de Unamuno: "Shake off this sadness, and recover your spirit."

4. *Breaking Apart: A Memoir of Divorce* by Wendy Swallow. "Why did you leave Daddy?" It's an obvious question for children of divorce, but as Swallow makes clear in this candid account of ending her fourteen-year marriage, the answer is complicated. Revisiting the pain and guilt that went with calling it quits, she argues that her decision still made sense and made her a stronger person. But don't tell that to the judge who, when granting the divorce, remarked, "If you can work this well together, I don't know why you can't stay married." Now *that* was helpful.

5. *Calling It Quits: Late-Life Divorce and Starting Over* by Deirdre Bair. It's no surprise to learn that more long-term marriages are hitting the rocks—just ask the AARP. Its surveys on postforty marital happiness, along with Bair's late-life divorce, inspired her to ask the question: What's the matter with these enduring relationships? Anecdotal it may be, but there's food for thought in hearing the dissatisfied tell their stories. Says Bair: Most marriages crumble gradually and from within, infidelity is

FLYING SOLO

Whenever I have needed to wash a man right out of my hair, I've taken a trip. A long trip. I've drowned my sorrows in some of the most romantic spots on earth, from Paris to Rio. Now I realize I should have tried Bali.

Who wouldn't head for that idyllic Indonesian isle after reading Victoria Q. Legg's "Savorings," one of the True Stories From Around the World collected in the 2007 edition of *The Best Women's Travel Writing*? Legg offers a steamy description of an erotic massage given to her by a Balinese masseuse named Tunla, a "master musician of the body."

Bali also crops up in Marybeth Bond's *Best Girlfriends Getaways Worldwide*. Ubud, the "epicenter of Bali's art, music and traditional dance scenes" and an "idyllic spa haven," is the site every fall of the Ubud Writers & Readers Festival. And if you stay at the pricey Amandari (rough translation: "peaceful angel") resort there, you can check off one of Patricia Schultz's *1,000 Places to See Before You Die*.

Theresa Rodriquez Williamson, founder of the online magazine for women travelers, TravelDiva.com, counts Bali as one of the *50 Best Places on Earth for a Girl to Travel Alone*. In *Fly Solo*, she provides a list of top ten extraordinary experiences found on the island (alas, the masseuse Tunla is not one of them). Number nine: Try some humming and omming. The island offers free yoga lessons.

Williams also recommends appropriate books to read before you go: *Island of Bali* by Miguel Covarrubias, *A Little Bit One o'Clock* by William Ingram, and *Eat, Pray, Love* by Elizabeth Gilbert. Novelist Gilbert went to the dreamy Indonesian island after her own breakup (Bali is the "love" portion of her memoir's title). But she warns against mentioning your divorce to the Balinese, if you happen to have had one. It will only worry them: "The only thing your solitude proves to them is your perilous dislocation from the grid. If you are a single woman traveling through Bali and somebody asks you, 'Are you married?' the best possible answer is: 'Not yet.' This is a polite way of saying, 'No,' while indicating your optimistic intentions to get that taken care of just as soon as you can. Even if you are eighty years old, or a lesbian, or a strident feminist nun, or an eighty-year-old strident feminist lesbian nun who has never been married and never intends to get married, the polite possible answer is still, 'Not yet.'"

~ Margo

less lethal than boredom, and healthy older wives aren't afraid to ask, "Is this all there is?"

6. *The Post-Birthday World* by Lionel Shriver. "In snooker, you learn the hard way that every shot is for keeps." So says Englishman Ramsey Acton, the sharp-shooting interloper in this novel about a love triangle—or is it a would-be love triangle? Shriver keeps you guessing as she shows the forty-two-year-old Irina McGovern agonizing over which shot to make, either to stay with her longtime live-in or opt for the delectable snooker champ. *Rashomon*-like, the novel imagines the same scenes with opposing outcomes as it lustily investigates the emotional terrain of romance.

7. *Lust, Caution: The Story* by Eileen Chang. Chang's canny attention to detail—the flashing of a diamond ring, the clacking of tiles—builds foreboding suspense in this short story (only

sixty-eight pages long). Set in 1940s Shanghai, it's about the thin line separating love and betrayal. Chia-chih, a young student actress, becomes part of an assassination plot: She is to seduce Mr. Yee, a philandering husband who is a pooh-bah in the Japanese occupational government, and lure him to an isolated spot. A lover's ultimate treachery? The shocking twist in the final pages will fuel plenty of book club discussion.

8. *The Sweet Potato Queens' Wedding Planner/Divorce Guide* by Jill Conner Browne. "Statistically speaking, 100 percent of all divorces begin with weddings," says Browne, Mississippi's self-appointed Sweet Potato Queen, in this hilarious two-in-one guide for brides and (when you flip it over) those on the other side of wedding bliss. If you haven't read any of this Southern humorist's outrageous books before, wear a seatbelt. And lots of sequins. Her salty-ass attitude and bawdy humor is all about empowering women. "It's gonna be all right," she consoles. "Tiaras on, butts out, tits up, and move on, darlin'."

9. *My Mistress's Sparrow Is Dead: Great Love Stories, From Chekhov to Munro* edited by Jeffrey Eugenides. In his introduction, Eugenides distinguishes between love and a love *story:* "Love stories depend on disappointment, on unequal births and feuding families, on matrimonial boredom and at least one cold heart." That hasn't been our experience (see 10 About Enduring Bonds), but we sure love the twenty-seven tales of doomed love he has gathered here. His title is inspired by Latin poet Catullus, the first to write about a personal love affair. Of course, like his mistress's sparrow, it ended badly.

10. *Deal Breakers: When to Work on a Relationship and When to Walk Away* by Dr. Bethany Marshall. Deal or no deal: To psychoanalyst Marshall, women need to negotiate romance as if it were a business. Her easy-to-digest guide helps decide whether a problem is surmountable or just "the tip of the misery iceberg." In her book, infidelity is not always a deal breaker, unless it's a pattern. Marshall identifies five personality types to help you define the problem and ask your significant other to change. If he says no, let him eat your dust.

TO KEEP THINGS HOT

1. *Classic Nasty: More Naughty Bits: A Rollicking Guide to Hot Sex in Great Books, From* The Iliad *to* The Corrections by Jack Murnighan. You may not read Great Literature for the dirty parts (any more than men read *Playboy* for the articles), but the scenes catalogued in Nerve.com columnist Murnighan's second volume prove the power of fiction to "stir the senses." But beware: He begins and ends with the story of the adulterous Paolo and Francesca from Dante's *Divine Comedy*, who were spurred on by reading a racy book and ended up in hell.

2. *The Sexual Life of Catherine M.* by Catherine Millet. "Some of the traits of my sexual personality support slight regressive tendencies," Millet writes in classic understatement in this international best seller, first published in the world's passion capital, Paris. A

BOOKS AS APHRODISIACS

The title of the first book that was given away as a gift is not known, but I'll bet it was a book of poetry, given by an incurable romantic to his lady love.

Books are natural aphrodisiacs. Just after getting married, I gave my first husband a book for Valentine's Day. His gift to me was the same book on Mexican art. We thought it was a sign that we were meant for each other. We didn't realize then that our book swap echoed an exchange between lovers that takes place every year in the Catalan capital of Barcelona. On April 23, known in Spain as El Diada de Sant Jordi, or St. George's Day, men throughout Spain traditionally give their sweethearts roses, the symbol of love, much like other cultures do on St. Valentine's Day. In 1923, however, a Catalan bookseller came up with a novel variation on that theme: Women were asked to return the gesture with a book. Now the day is known both as *el Dia de la Rosa* (Day of the Rose) and *el Dia de la Libro* (Day of the Book).

The clever Catalan bookseller said he chose the day for book giving because of its special place in literary history—the date marks the death of both Miguel de Cervantes and William Shakespeare. Unfortunately, anyone who received a book about the history of the calendar on St. George's Day would discover that the linking of Cervantes and Shakespeare in death involves a sleight of hand. Cervantes actually died ten days earlier than Shakespeare. At the time of these two literary giants' deaths, the Spanish used the Gregorian calendar, while the British calculated time with the Julian. The Calendar Act of 1752 put Britain in sync with the continent, the first day of the year was changed from March 25 to January 1—and the ten-day gap between the two nations disappeared. But why ruin a great coincidence with facts?

> Now, every year on the Day of the Book, booksellers line the streets selling their wares in outdoor booths and cafes. Bookstores host appearances by local authors and marathon readings of Cervantes' *Don Quixote*. More than 400,000 books are bought and given away as tokens of respect and love.
>
> I hope a lot of them are poetry books. My first marriage lasted ten years; those Mexican art books we gave each other have long disappeared. But I still have the book of poetry my high school boyfriend gave me: T. S. Eliot's *Complete Poems and Plays: 1909–1950*.
>
> **~ Margo**

literary critic, Millet covers it all—fantasies, group sex, visits to the dentist (guess how she pays to maintain those pearly whites). "Having never attributed any sacred value to sex," she says, "I have never felt the need to shut it up in a tabernacle as (most likely) do those who criticize me for robbing it of all mystery." Yow!

3. *That Summer in Paris* by Abha Dawesar. Speaking of the passion capital, in this steamy novel about sex and literary inspiration, Prem Rustum, a Nobel Prize–winning Indian author, meets a young woman when she evokes his name on a dating website (even aging writers know how to google). Impulsively he follows Maya to Paris, where she goes to write her first novel. There his passions are awakened, both in his personal life and in his work. Yours will be, too, by New Delhi author Dawesar's lush prose: "Everything in the (patisserie) was glistening, soft, jellylike, moist, rich, and luscious . . . dying for a lick."

4. *The Sex-Starved Marriage: A Couple's Guide to Boosting Their Marriage Libido* by Michele Weiner Davis. Not in the mood? Well, join the club, according to marriage therapist Davis, who sizes up partners on both sides of the desire divide. She says the cure for a mismatch starts with good listening to thaw a cold fish and warm touch to soothe the horny toad. No steamy stuff, just guidance for how you and your significant other can get it on without getting on each other's nerves. Key point: Sex isn't just about sex; it's about emotional intimacy.

5. *The Vampire Lestat* by Anne Rice. Like all vampire tales, beginning with Bram Stoker's *Dracula,* this gothic account of the life of Lestat de Lioncourt taps into dark sexual longings. Vampires never die, so neither do their desires. But where past vampires elicited horror, Rice's bloodsucker, who relates his own story, is sympathetic and alluring. Blond, bisexual, and endlessly libidinous, he is a taboo breaker who struggles with his murderous nature. Operating under the cover of darkness, he is excitingly romantic, a "Gentleman Death in silk and lace, come to put out the candles."

6. *The Secret to Understanding Women's Hidden Passions* by Gillian Holloway. Do you dream of making love to a faceless man? Or to an old boyfriend? Or maybe to Tom Cruise? Dream researcher Holloway describes all these scenarios and dozens more in this survey of women's sexual dreams and fantasies. But her interpretations—and list of symbols commonly reoccurring in women's exotic dreams, from affairs to zombies—are only meant to be a springboard for your own dream work: "Start a dream journal. One of the best ways to fulfill passion is to understand your dreams."

7. *The X List: The National Society of Film Critics' Guide to the Movies That Turn Us On, From* It Happened One Night *to* Last Tango in Paris *to* Beyond the Valley of the Dolls . . . *and Beyond!* edited by Jami Bernard. Explicit sex scenes aren't the only cinematic turn-ons, according to this compendium of forty film critics. "Words in movies can be as or more erotic," says William Wolf, citing Molly's soliloquy in the 1967 movie version of James Joyce's *Ulysses.* For Bernard it is the musical *Bye Bye Birdie* that "heaves with sexual subtext." Put on a happy face, indeed.

8. *Married Lust: 10 Secrets of Long Lasting Desire* by Pamela Lister and *Redbook* magazine. "Sex. Passion. Marriage. And learning how to put all three together in the same sentence." That's the agenda of this book from a popular magazine for young marrieds, which used two Internet surveys to ask ten thousand men and women between twenty-five and thirty-five about their sex lives. How do you set the stage for love when the embers of desire need a blowtorch to be rekindled? Not by accident, that's for sure. Here are some new moves and ways to set the mood.

9. *The Best American Erotica* series edited by Susie Bright. Bright, a columnist for *Playboy*, found a tantalizing theme for this fourteenth edition: "war and lust between generations." Among her selections: excerpts from Alicia Erian's "Towelhead" (a Lebanese-American teenager paired with a racist Gulf War vet) and Octavia Butler's "Fledging" (a new twist on the vampire tale),

as well as Shanna Germain's "Entry Point" (a married couple's passion sparked by seeing their grown daughter's example). Bright even boldly includes a scene from Jessica Cutler's controversial *Washingtonienne*, based on the former intern's real-life sex scandal that rocked the nation's capital.

10. *America Unzipped: In Search of Sex and Satisfaction* by Brian Alexander. MSNBC.com's "Sexploration" columnist reports on everything from a fetish convention to a sex club in this amusing look at America's sexual underbelly. His conclusions? Most Americans "don't enter into polyamorous relationships, have probably never heard of shibari, and might think bukkake is a beer from Japan." But "sexual experimentation, sometimes radical experimentation, has become a mainstream pursuit." The problem? Kinkiness, sold as a mass-market product, has become boring. "Acceptance dampens the frisson that makes taboo delicious." Who wants *Delta of Venus* if it isn't forbidden?

TO HELP YOU THINK MORE LIKE A GUY

1. *The Road* by Cormac McCarthy. "Now call down your dark and your cold and be damned." This spare line sums up the grim postapocalyptic universe occupied by one unnamed man and his son as they trek through a wasted landscape in hope of salvation. Against this hard, spare backdrop, McCarthy illuminates the singular task that has defined the male species—and brought out

the best and worst in humanity—since the beginning of time. "My job is to take care of you," the man tells the boy. "I was appointed to do that by God. I will kill anyone who touches you."

2. *Where Men Hide* by James B. Twitchell. Men hide in basements and garages, in deer camps and boxing rings, in strip clubs and snuggeries, or in plain sight on their recliners. Why do they need to hide? To escape the pressures of being male, says Twitchell, a University of Florida professor whose essays are paired here with Ken Ross's photographs of men's hidey-holes. They don't hide because they despise women, he says. They just need places where they can be alone or in the company of other men who don't ask them why they need to hide.

3. *This Boy's Life* by Tobias Wolff. In this memoir, novelist Wolff crawls into his boyhood skin, recreating with perfect pitch the mindset of a troubled kid. He's troubled for good reason: His divorced mother has a taste for controlling men. His stepfathers link love to violence. But Wolff doesn't play the blame game. Instead, he tells his story with the clear-headedness of a man who has escaped such restricting views of what it is to be male: "My first stepfather used to say that what I didn't know would fill a book. Well, here it is."

4. *The Life and Times of the Thunderbolt Kid: A Memoir* by Bill Bryson. Here's childhood without the angst. That's the Middle America Bryson recalls in this memoir about growing up in Iowa during the 1950s. His wholesome and wide-eyed view of the world seldom waivers—except, of course, when a friend helps him talk his way into the stripper's tent at the state fair by claiming Bryson, who was too young to enter, had an inoperable brain tumor. When "she leaned out over the audience and gave a ten-second twirl of her tassels," Bryson writes, "I thought I had died and that this was heaven."

5. *Breath: A Novel* by Tim Winton. The tumultuous ride toward manhood is both literal and figurative for Bruce, the narrator of this steamy novel by Australian writer Winton. Looking back, he recalls his teen years surfing giant waves with his risk-loving buddy, Loonie, and their adult sidekick, Sando. Wrapped in the dangers and insecurities of his age, Bruce challenges himself: "Was I serious? Could I do something gnarly, or was I just ordinary?" Stand back as the "weird, reptilian" psyche of a confused and sexually charged young man turns thought into action.

6. *Love Is a Mix Tape: Life and Loss, One Song at a Time* by Rob Sheffield. Paying tribute to his five-year marriage, Sheffield describes how two rock critics—he and his wife, Renée—built a beautiful relationship around music and each other. When she died suddenly from a pulmonary embolism at age thirty-one, he was left with his tape cassettes, iPod, and the same feeling expressed by another young widower, Ralph Waldo Emerson: "I grieve that grief can teach me nothing." Here's the kind of sensitive guy you can bring home to Mother. She'll offer him condolences and compliment you for your good taste.

7. *Lay of the Land* by Richard Ford. The self-absorbed Frank Bascombe of Ford's earlier novel "The Sportswriter" reappears as a real estate agent on the Jersey Shore, nearly divorced for the second time and dealing with prostate cancer. The pre-9/11 landscape is full of strip malls and personal striving, and Frank's interior landscape shows a man at the point "when life is a destination more than a journey and when who you feel yourself to be is pretty much how people will remember you when you've croaked." This is no midlife crisis, just Frank calling 'em as he sees 'em.

8. *The Bastard on the Couch: 27 Men Try Really Hard to Explain Their Feelings About Love, Loss, Fatherhood, and Freedom* edited by Daniel Jones. First came *The Bitch in the House,* a collection of clever essays reflecting contemporary womanhood that was edited by Cathi Hanauer. Then Hanauer's husband said, "I can do that, too!" And he has, attracting funny, self-suspecting types who may dream of hot weekends in Vegas but know that, as one contributor puts it, "the guy at the craps table gambling with his rent money is an idiot."

9. *Quiet Strength: The Principles, Practices, & Priorities of a Winning Life* by Tony Dungy and Nathan Whitaker. Even football widows can love the mild-mannered Dungy. Here, he looks at his ups (the first African-American coach to win a Super Bowl) and downs (the heartbreaking loss of his son to suicide) with equal humility. Placing family over fame and God over everything, he's more interested in winning the game of life than on the field: "Football is just a game. It's not family. It's not a way of life. It doesn't provide any sort of intrinsic meaning. It's just football."

10. *Stiffed: The Betrayal of the American Man* by Susan Faludi. Faludi held plenty of preconceived ideas about men before she began this exhaustive study: They feel entitled; they're anti-women. But after interviewing hundreds of underemployed, contracted-out, and laid-off men, diminished by mass culture, her stereotypes were shattered. Men, she concludes, are understandably confused by a society that sends mixed messages about how to be a man. But her own message is clear: "Their task is not to figure out how to be masculine—rather, their masculinity lies in figuring out how to be human."

VI

HOME, WORK, & TAKING CARE

William Trevor puts his finger right on it. Essential to Jane Austen's six great novels was an era which "so valued appearances—and manners and style—that their valuation became the very heart of the age," he writes in the introduction to the Oxford World Classic edition to *Pride and Prejudice*.

Snobs, in other words, make great copy. To be a good writer, you need to be something of a sociologist, astute to the pretensions and vices that rule the day.

This was the spirit Austen brought to her work. And apparently she didn't need to travel beyond the breakfast table to find good material. After her death, family members tried to tamp down the subversiveness of her work and preserve her for posterity as everyone's favorite maiden aunt.

Yet Austen was anything but the gentle spinster. Just months before she died, she wrote, "Pictures of perfection make me sick and wicked."

The Austen who wrote such perceptive novels possessed a piercing intelligence and enough courage to turn down a perfectly decent marriage proposal at a time when women were programmed to take the best offer. Rather than marry a man she didn't love, she focused on writing fiction that exposed the hypocrisies of her world and, by displacement, give modern readers a perspective on their own.

In this section the Babes look at the way we live now. We spotlight the customs and expectations that frame how we spend our time, energy, and dollars. Not unlike the rector's daughter who peeled the lid off the social code of nineteenth-century England, the authors featured here have turned on their radar and, yes, their bullshit detectors, to ask some pointed questions (who needs a house the size of a hunting lodge?), confirm some eternal verities (home cooking is better when it's seasoned with love), scrutinize workplace etiquette (get your eyes off my e-mail), and commit to the idea that we're all in this together, regardless of creed or color.

The affluence of the past few decades has had more benefits than we can count. But hold on! Affluence has bred a thirst for acquisition, and this thirst has dulled the senses to other things that matter—relationships, ideas, the arts. There's no harm in drinking lattes and knowing your way around the mall. But let's put things in perspective.

As global warming looms and gas prices zoom, don't we need to live as consciously as we can and not according to a list of "gottas" created by our consumer culture?

TV host Johnny Carson famously said that he'd been both rich and poor, and rich was better. Although lacking Carson's experience with both sides, how can the Babes argue? But this much we know: A well-padded bank account is only one defense against the problems that complicate people's lives. So this section also looks at sorrows to which no one is immune: illness, grief, disability, substance abuse, poverty.

These subjects seem far removed from the prissy word etiquette. But not that far: Ceremonies exist to help us cope with those moments when we go into emotional overdrive. Weddings, funerals, and even that modern invention, the intervention—somehow, in such circumstances, it helps to have a script. What's less scripted, as you'll see from the books ahead, is how to get along in a world that's increasingly multicultural and still rattled by 9/11.

Comparing our world to Jane Austen's, it's sometimes difficult to draw a straight line. Partly that's because the American melting pot changes the nature of this country's novels and nonfiction, as follows:

For the past two centuries, the Brits have honed the comedy of manners to a fine art. Because they live on an island where someone can identify your social status by the first words that come out of your mouth, their writers have a readymade opportunity to pit upstairs against downstairs and play for a laugh.

America is too big and diffuse for that. Although satire is no stranger here—this is, after all, the land of Mark Twain—humorists seem outgunned when stacked up against the stories of the eager and desperate who have made it or failed on these shores. Striving defines this nation of immigrants and its literature, nowhere more clearly than in Theodore Dreiser's 1927 novel, *An American Tragedy*—fiction based on the true story of a young man who killed his pregnant lover when she got in the way of his ambition and chance to woo the boss's daughter.

But earnestness (Dale Carnegie's *How to Make Friends and Influence People*) and humor (Paul Fussell's *Class: A Guide Through the American Status System*) have been used to show all sides of the American dream, as well. The potential for social and economic mobility creates a culture of optimists who are not only generous to themselves, but also to others.

Jane Austen couldn't have asked for better material.

THAT FEED THE NESTING INSTINCT

1. *House Thinking: A Room by Room Look at How We Live* by Winifred Gallagher. Forget "leafing through magazines or collecting paint chips." Getting your home just right is not about how it looks, but how you feel in it, says Gallagher, who emphasizes the power surroundings have on moods and behavior. Here, she goes through each room of your house, from the entrance hall to the basement, from your child's room to your office, to help you think about creating a home that is a place that both shelters and fascinates: "a womb with a view."

2. *To Hell With All That: Loving and Loathing Our Inner Housewife* by Caitlin Flanagan. Elaborate white weddings are back. Martha Stewart has glamorized "cleaning and ironing and looking after chickens." Do modern women long to return to the time of the "Happy Housewife"? No, but when the '50s turned into the '60s, women advanced but they also left something behind, says Flanagan in these funny and wise essays. Nesters or stock investors? "Whichever decision a woman makes, she will lose something of incalculable value."

3. *House Lust: America's Obsession with Our Homes* by Daniel McGinn. The good news is that you no longer need to be upper crust to own your own home. The bad news is that, for the two-thirds of Americans who do, it may no longer be such a hot investment. The average 1950 house contained 983 square feet, which in today's supersized abodes accommodates the master bath. Such excess paved the driveway to the eco-chic countertrend, popularized by Sarah Susanka's *The Not So Big House*: "Dollars are a very poor measure of anything that matters."

4. *House* by Tracy Kidder. Americans' love affair with real estate isn't abstract here, in Kidder's classic saga about one couple's adventures building themselves a home in Amherst, Massachusetts. By now their house is nearly a quarter-century old—time for an upgrade!—but Kidder's story remains fresh because it's focused on relationships, not bath fixtures. The architect "brings pretty pictures," the builder says. "I've gotta bring reality." You watch tensions mount along with the price tag, but in the end the owners forget the labor pains. If you have enough cash and stamina—big if—custom building is where it's at.

5. *The Book of Old Houses* by Sarah Graves. Homicide mixes with home repair in this tale of murder and mayhem, part of a series starring Jacobia "Jake" Tiptree, a funny, gun-savvy, former money manager for the mob. Like her creator Sarah Graves (a good pen name for a mystery writer), Jake is restoring an 1823 Federal house in Eastpoint, Maine, which accounts for some of the mayhem. Following such punning titles as *Tool & Die* and *Mallets Aforethought*, this eleventh in the series offers suspense, Down East lore, and a rising body count—not to mention useful home-repair tips.

6. *The Big House: A Century in the Life of an American Summer House* by George Howe Colt. The vacation home as cultural signifier: In this memoir, Colt returns to the Cape Cod "cottage" where his kin spent summers throughout the twentieth century— one with eight gables and eleven bedrooms. Such is the way well-bred people understate their riches, and in this tender tribute you see not just the rise and fall of one family's wealth but the sensibilities of an entire class. Apparently even when you attend the finest schools, you're not immune to heartbreak and financial retraction.

7. *Keeping the House* by Ellen Barker. Barker's novel is also about choices. Dolly has been striving to be the perfect '50s housewife, complete with matching aprons and rotating recipes. But something is missing. Discovering a run-down mansion in her Wisconsin town and the story of the hapless women who lived there gives her a jolt: "Forget creating a home for her husband à la Donna Reed. She would be strong-minded and disagreeable like Bette Davis." She still stands by her man but concludes: Keeping the house doesn't need to keep you from your dreams.

8. *A Perfect Mess: The Hidden Benefits of Disorder: How Crammed Closets, Cluttered Offices, and On-the-Fly Planning Make the World a Better Place* by Eric Abrahamson and David H. Freedman. "There's already too much emphasis on and advice about how to get organized," say these authors, who offer a captivating antidote for those whose bookshelves are cluttered with anticlutter books: Embrace mess. Neatness has costs both to your pocketbook (organization is expensive) and psyche: "It's the optional, extraneous items we leave lying around that bear the stamp of our quirky inner selves." Are you listening, Felix Unger?

9. *Braving Home: Dispatches from the Underwater Town, the Lava-Side Inn, and Other Extreme Locales* by Jake Halpern. In this engaging piece of Americana, the young Halpern showcases a set of geographically diverse homeowners dedicated to living in hazardous or bizarre locales. His cast may be "the sort of diehard Americans you'd see on the six o'clock news and promptly dismiss as nuts." But on closer inspection they evoke Halpern's envy and our respect for defining home as their source of history, tradition, and "an almost organic sense of permanence."

10. The Mitford series by Jan Karon. This is comfort reading that defines home as bigger than four walls: nine bestselling books that revolve around the North Carolina mountain community that gives the series its name. If you have small-town roots, this place may feel more benign than the real thing, but that's the charm of it, after all. "Mitford takes care of its own," to quote the good mayor, and Father Tim Kavanagh, the town's thirtysomething Episcopal priest, puts those words into action as he copes with his own problems, his parishioners, and a woman named Cynthia. Start anywhere.

THAT PUT YOU ON THE GARDEN PATH

1. *The Garden of Reading: An Anthology of 20th-century Short Fiction About Gardens and Gardeners* edited by Michele Slung. The Bible begins with a garden story, Slung notes, introducing this anthology of twenty-four garden-related stories. Even the word anthology has its roots in the garden, combining the Greek words *anthos* (flower) and *legein* (to gather). With this gathering, Slung flings you a fragrant bouquet, mixing James Thurber's witty "See No Weevil" and Edna O'Brien's touching "Christmas Roses" with Stephen King's horrific "Lawnmower Man" and Colette's sensual "Grape Harvest." How did she do it? It's all in the pruning.

2. *Botany of Desire: A Plant's Eye View of the World* by Michael Pollan. Killer kudzu they're not, yet the apple, tulip, potato, and marijuana have wrapped their destiny around human progress and, as Pollan would have it, reveal "the great reciprocal web" of life. Flowers, it turns out, jumpstarted evolution. Apples actually fall far from the tree, needing grafts to replicate. The potato industry makes Pollan a convert to organic farming, while pot's place in history may have been to mask childbirth pain and erase it from a new mom's memory. So there's the web, in a nutshell.

3. *Pilgrim at Tinker Creek* by Annie Dillard. This Pulitzer Prize–winning ode to nature and the interior life, first published in 1974, covers topics as diverse as the weather, other books, and the secret world in the stream near Dillard's Virginia home. All that's required is to "hush the noise of useless interior babble" and truly see the objects of your curiosity. "Don't believe them when they tell you how economical and thrifty nature is," she writes. "This deciduous business alone is a radical scheme, the brainchild of a deranged manic-depressive with limitless capital. Extravagance! Nature will try anything once."

4. *Animal, Vegetable, Miracle: A Year of Food Life* by Barbara Kingsolver, with Steven L. Hopp and Camille Kingsolver. "We're a nation with an eating disorder, and we know it," says novelist Kingsolver, who turns this memoir into a position paper for using farm-grown goods as the cure. When she and her family relocated from Tucson to an Appalachian hollow, they agreed to either raise or grow what they ate or try to know who was doing it for them. Husband Hopp contributes his background in biology to this blueprint for eating locally, no matter where you are.

5. *Of Flowers & a Village: An Entertainment for Flower Lovers* by Wilfrid Blunt. This epistolary novel, first published in 1963, places you in the mind and heart of an archetype, the English gardening devotee, and is sheer delight for anyone who sees the humor in a sign that says, "Beware of the *Scolopendrium!*" (It's a fern. Get the joke?) Blunt, renowned as a botany scholar, adopts the role of a godfather writing to young Flora (more Brit

wit) about his exploits in the village of Dewbery, where life revolves around seeds, flowers, a gentleman's erudition, and, of
course, tea.

6. *Gardening at the Dragon's Gate: At Work in the Wild and Cultivated World* by Wendy Johnson. Gardeners are pilgrims, says
Buddhist Johnson, who has spent thirty years blending spiritual
practice with an obsession for growing things at the 115-acre
Green Gulch Farm Zen Center near San Francisco. You can appreciate her gardening know-how without sharing her belief
system, but brace yourself: Johnson's lyrical prose and mindfulness are intoxicating. When she advises, "Let the earth carry you
forward," it seems like the right prescription for much more
than gardening.

7. *My Garden* by Jamaica Kincaid. Born in Antigua and transplanted to Vermont, novelist Kincaid built her first garden beds
in the shape of Caribbean islands. In these rambling reflections
of a late-blooming gardener, she waxes on about seed catalogues
and heirloom bulbs, describes a trip to China in search of more
exotic plants, and charmingly revels in her horticultural failures.
Her wisteria blooms out of turn. Her pansies "are committing
suicide, in desperate need of deadheading." But she is ecstatic:
"Oh, the deliciousness of complaining about nothing of any
consequence."

8. *Orchid Fever: A Horticultural Tale of Love, Lust, and Lunacy*
by Eric Hansen and *The Orchid Thief: A True Story of Beauty and
Obsession* by Susan Orlean. Two books on orchids? Isn't that

overkill? Not for those with orchid fever, a condition brought on by those fragrant and sometimes elusive flowers. Orlean's version inspired the wacky movie *Adaptation*; Hansen's account has the best factoid: *Salepi dondurma,* or fox-testicle ice cream, is a Turkish delicacy made from the dried tubers of wild orchids. Beware: Just reading these entertaining books about orchids could raise your temperature.

9. *The Hive: The Story of the Honey Bee and Us* by Bee Wilson. Mormons do it. Masons do it. Even heavyweight champions do it. Obsess about bees, that is. This honey of a book—yes, the author's name really is Bee, for Beatrice—drips with fascinating facts about the busy creatures buzzing around your garden and their golden product. Muhammad Ali, after promising to sting like a bee, drank a honey-based potion before his fights. Leo Tolstoy was a "beekeeper-sage." Oh, and contrary to the popular Cole Porter ditty, most bees *don't* do it.

10. *Flower Confidential: The Good, the Bad and the Beautiful* by Amy Stewart. Stewart's stories are so entertaining, you'll hardly notice that you're learning bunches about the multibillion-dollar floral industry—the breeding, growing and selling of cut flowers. Americans buy more flowers than Big Macs, she tells us, and they aren't your mother's garden variety. Show-stopping lilies. Dark purple carnations. Scentless petunias. And maybe, someday, a blue rose. Modern flowers are the "outcome of our tinkering and manipulation," says Stewart. But, an unabashed flower lover, she's not complaining: "In some cases the results are glorious."

THAT HOLD THE WINNING RECIPE

1. *The Warmest Room in the House: How the Kitchen Became the Heart of the Twentieth-Century American Home* by Steven Gdula. Technology, not taste, has driven changes in how America cooks and eats. Innovations in food manufacture and home appliances explain the move to store-made bread, frozen foods, and even Pop Tarts, Gdula claims—not exactly a recipe for gourmet dining, but here's the good news: Starting with Depression-era ethnic cooks who fed their needy neighbors, he claims, the country's culinary horizons expanded exponentially. Kung pao chicken, anyone?

2. *The Girl With No Shadow* by Joanne Harris. In Harris's novel *Chocolat,* Vianne Rocher seduced an entire French village with the intoxicating scent of her confections. In this sequel, she turns up in Paris's Montmartre district four years later, again running a chocolate shop, but sans the enchantment. She wants a "normal" life for her daughters. But when an alluring yet dangerous figure in lollipop shoes named Zozie blows in, Vianne learns you don't have to live without magic. You just need to distinguish the good from the bad. Once again chocolate leads the way.

3. *Choice Cuts: A Savory Selection of Food Writing From Around the World and Throughout History* edited by Mark Kurlansky. "Tell me what you eat, and I shall tell you what you are," said the legendary French food writer Jean Anthelme Brillat-Savarin. That sums up the essence of this savory sampler, which includes such tidbits as Marjorie Kinnan Rawlings's belief in the hot biscuit as the cornerstone of Southern hospitality and A. J. Liebling's assertion that vodka is the "ideal intoxicant for the drinker who wants no reminder of how hurt Mother would be if she knew what he was doing."

4. *Poet of the Appetites: The Lives and Loves of M.F.K. Fisher* by Joan Reardon. Fisher wrote about food "not with the seriousness of a culinary historian, but with every intention to seduce," says Reardon. Yet Mary Francis was not only a Scheherazade of the table. In her memoirs, Fisher also whipped up fantastic tales about her life: "I do not lie. But I have never seen any reason to be dull." Here, Reardon peeks behind the façade. But, don't worry, it's a portrait served up with plenty of admiration for the writer who once described how to cook a wolf.

5. *Alice Waters and Chez Panisse: The Romantic, Impractical, Ultimately Brilliant Making of a Food Revolution* by Thomas McNamee. First came Julia (see *My Life in France* in 10 with Signature Style). Then came Alice Waters, another Sorbonne alum, whose name is synonymous with fresh ingredients and imaginative cooking. This twenty-something "without a moment of self-doubt" lacked fiscal restraint but not gumption when she opened the Berkeley restaurant Chez Panisse in 1971. In this account, lovers come and go, but Waters's influence remains a constant as she makes eating a matter of lifestyle.

6. *Comfort Me With Apples: More Adventures at the Table* by Ruth Reichl. Start here or backtrack to Reichl's earlier *Tender at*

JOY IN THE KITCHEN

My mom, who died in 1998, was always an ambivalent housewife. But she was a great cook, and I take a trip down memory lane every time I use one of her handwritten recipes or open a copy of the cookbook that was her kitchen staple, *The Joy of Cooking* by Irma S. Rombauer.

American cooking has a long and polyglot history, thanks to our immigrant heritage. In 1896, Fannie Farmer standardized measurements in *The Boston Cooking-School Cookbook,* and from there the race was on: Other cooks, both professional and not, began publishing comprehensive texts, Rombauer among them. With minimal culinary training, she got her start after being asked to teach a few classes to fellow parishioners at her Unitarian church in St. Louis, Missouri. In 1931, she took her life savings and self-published three-thousand copies of her collection of five hundred tested recipes, which included the top selling point, her user-friendly commentary. Continually updated by family members—first her daughter, Marion Becker, and then grandson, Ethan Becker—in 1995 the New York Public Library singled it out as the only cookbook among its picks for the most influential books of the twentieth century.

My mother and mother-in-law would both concur.

In addition to the 1940s edition that these two wonderful women received when they were young marrieds, I own two *Joys*—a well-worn, jacketless copy that marks my first ventures into the kitchen in the '70s, and the "All New, All Purpose" edition, first published in 1997. The newest one I still use, because it reflects the way we eat now. But occasionally I thumb through the yellowed pages of my oldest copy, taking a trip back to the tastes and aromas of a good cook's kitchen. My mother made the best apple pie you'd ever find, and I don't want to forget it.

~ Ellen

the Bone. Either way, you'll discover how Alice Waters and the Berkeley food scene figured in Reichl's rise through the food world, first as a restaurant critic and then as editor of *Gourmet* magazine. "Food!" her mother said dismissively early on, "all you write about is food." But Reichl countered, "Writing about restaurants doesn't have to be different from writing a novel." Her memoirs, like her reviews, prove her point, blending truth-telling, good taste, and the occasional recipe.

7. *The Book of Salt* by Monique Truong. After reading a reference in *The Alice B. Toklas Cookbook* to a Vietnamese cook that Toklas and her companion writer Gertrude Stein hired in Paris in the 1920s, Truong imagines that chef: Binh, a gay immigrant whose succulent meals and peculiar way of speaking (repeating and compressing his words) inspires the duo. Binh narrates this spicy glimpse into the eccentric household on the Rue de Fleurus, where even a common word like salt takes on layers of meaning: "What kind? Kitchen, sweat, tears, or the sea. Madame, they are not all the same."

8. *Rosewater and Soda Bread* by Marsha Mehran. Mix three beautiful Iranian sisters, Persian food, and the colorful denizens of a cabbage-eating Irish village. Add flashes of Iranian and Irish history and a dash of philosophy about clashing cultures. Those were the winning ingredients for *Pomegranate Soup,* Mehran's first installment of the Ballinacroagh series. In this sequel, she revisits the Aminpour sisters at the Babylon Café in Ireland's County Mayo, this time, as her title suggests, offering both Persian and Irish recipes to her tale. The result? A winning blend of good storytelling and great ideas for dinner.

9. *Broccoli and Other Tales of Food and Love* by Lara Vapnyar. Love and food intersect in these short stories by the Russian author of *There Are Jews in My House*. The love is mostly of the disappointing variety, with lovers "seduced and abandoned," like the bunches of broccoli in the title story. But the food, lushly described, transports the characters, émigrés like their creator, to the lands they left behind: borscht "steaming, bursting with colors" and "diverse aromas of curry, ginger, garlic and basil." Added bonus: a roundup of recipes based on all that fictional food.

10. *Climbing the Mango Trees: A Memoir of a Childhood in India* by Madhur Jaffrey. Talk about a multicultural experience: In this food-infused tale from cookbook author Jaffrey, she recalls how her English-educated father watched the BBC while her Hindi-speaking mother sat on a mat, praying. Yet theirs was a happy union, and in her large, wealthy family, the only real blow was her sister's life-changing illness. ("My mother came in daily with a plate holding two beautiful *badaam ki golis*. We said little, just quietly dripped our salty tears over the sweet almond balls.") Blending the sweet and sour, Jaffrey gets the flavors just right.

FOR THE HOSTESS WITH THE MOSTESS

1. *Party of the Century: The Fabulous Story of Truman Capote and His Black and White Ball* by Deborah Davis. Capote's *bal* *masqué* marked a turning point in social history, says Davis in this dishy tell-all book on the bash. Linking murder and celebrity (the star-studded event was paid for by the proceeds of *In Cold Blood*), the party ushered in the era of "media madness," as one guest noted. Manhattan's Plaza Hotel provided a secret entrance for guests wanting to evade the rush of paparazzi out front. But not a single person, "famous or unfamous," used it.

2. *Everybody Was So Young: Gerald and Sara Murphy: A Lost Generation Love Story* by Amanda Vaill. In this absorbing account of life among American expatriates in the '20s, Vaill recreates the excitement the Murphys generated, the tragedy they endured (two young sons lost to illness), and, oh, their wonderful parties. When the Murphys welcomed you at the Villa America on the French Riviera, it was an invitation to experience life as a work of art. In turn, the sociable couple inspired the work of their cosmopolitan friends, including F. Scott Fitzgerald's *Tender Is the Night* and Picasso's *Woman in White*.

3. *The Hours* by Michael Cunningham. A novel about three separate days in the life of three different women is Cunningham's homage to Woolf's classic novel *Mrs. Dalloway*. Remember Mrs. D.? She decided to buy the flowers herself as she spent the day preparing for a party. Here she comes to life under Cunningham's hand, provides refuge for the unhappy, cake-baking Laura Brown, and is inspiration for her latter-day counterpart, Clarissa Vaughan, who appreciates the need to have "an hour here or there when our lives seem, against all expectation, to burst open and give us everything we've ever imagined."

4. *Bridget Jones's Diary* by Helen Fielding. When Bridget Jones meets up with Mark Darcy at the New Year's Day Turkey Curry Buffet in this hilarious send-up of singleton angst, we know we are in for a modernized version of the infamous hookup between that other Mr. Darcy and Elizabeth Bennett in *Pride and Prejudice*. "It struck me as pretty ridiculous to be called Mr. Darcy and to stand on your own looking snooty at a party," Bridget muses. "It's like being called Heathcliff and insisting on spending the entire evening in the garden, shouting 'Cathy' and banging your head against a tree."

5. *White Teeth* by Zadie Smith. Smith's characters also are thrown together at a party in this sprawling novel about an exuberant marriage that crosses barriers of race and age. This time, it's love at first sight. After failing to commit suicide, Archie Jones, a white working class Englishman, looks up and sees a banner heralding an End of the World Party. There he meets Clara Bowden, walking "down the stairs in slow motion, surrounded by afterglow and fuzzy lighting." A Jamaican less than half his age, she's "not only the most beautiful woman he ever met but the most comforting."

6. *Mrs. Clean Jean's Housekeeping With Kids* by Tara Aronson. Okay, be honest: The hardest part about having people over is not the cooking, it's the cleaning. If you have kids, their clutter magnifies the problem. This book will put you in fighting trim for all comers and give you more time to cook and arrange the flowers. Aronson doesn't miss a beat, going so far as to advise your own built-in wrinkle shield, a "scrunch and release" test before you buy any clothing. She also recommends allowances. Yes, children should do their part because they live there, too, but spare yourself the arguing, and you'll have more time to party.

7. *How's Your Drink? Cocktail, Culture, and the Art of Drinking Well* by Eric Felten. Even if you don't imbibe, this little gem about the rise and fall of cocktail fashions will put you in the partying mood. Yes, there are recipes (manhattans, martinis, etc.), but more fun is the historical and literary context this *Wall Street Journal* columnist provides. Who would have thought that the old-fashioned fell out of favor because of John Updike? Apparently that drink was the choice of Janice Angstrom, the wife in *Rabbit, Run,* who made it a turn-off because she was a drunk, and a sloppy one at that.

8. *Angry Housewives Eating Bon Bons* by Lorna Landvik. Liquor is quicker, and candy—well, it's just a metaphor for the fellowship found in this story about five neighbors in Minneapolis whose friendship begins with their Angry Housewives book club. For them, hospitality means not just hostessing the monthly meeting but also being there for each other through life's assorted traumas. A whole slew of reading becomes the backdrop for their thirty years of living. Secrets, divorces, illness—all fuel the underlying idea that together these women are catalysts for each other's growth.

9. *Being Dead Is No Excuse: The Official Southern Ladies' Guide to Hosting the Perfect Funeral* by Gayden Metcalfe and Charlotte Hays. These two belles from Greenville leave no stone unturned

in preparing for that final goodbye. From songs For the Well Bred Dead Person to the best funeral food ("Nothing whispers sympathy quite like a frozen-pea casserole with canned bean sprouts and mushroom soup"), their advice is, well, dead on. The first thing a Southern lady does when she gets the sad news that someone in the family has died? Polish the silver, of course. "A nice funeral is good for everyone."

10. *I Like You: Hospitality Under the Influence* by Amy Sedaris. Relax—entertaining can be fun, says Sedaris, sister of David, who displays the same offbeat sense of humor in this guide to feeding and caring for your guests. Some of her ideas are over the top, but laugh them off, following her lead. For Sedaris, attitude is the most important part of hospitality. "When a major setback occurs, don't snap your bean," she advises. "Make a joke out of the situation, turn it around. Take a snapshot of the rump roast you just dropped and send everyone a copy the next day."

THAT CELEBRATE YOUR BRILLIANT CAREER

1. *Mustang Sallies: Success Secrets of Women Who Refuse to Run With the Herd* by Fawn Germer. Mustang Sallies are women who "use power, not fear it," says journalist Germer. Here, she tells the secrets of dozens of successful women, from Washington's Hillary Clinton to Wall Street's Carly Fiorina. The best advice?

Keep asking questions. Meg Whitman did when she became CEO of eBay: "I'm sure a lot of technology executives thought, 'God, she doesn't know a lot,' but when you ask, they want to help you understand."

2. *Lessons of a Lipstick Queen* by Poppy King. At eighteen, King launched a multimillion-dollar company selling matte lipstick. In this guide, she tells her story and gives you practical advice about finding your own idea ("Take very seriously any sentence starting with 'I wish'"). She also gives tips on how to research, finance, and market that dream. "There is no one determining factor, no guarantee, no variable, measurement, formula, magic, fact, or secret that you don't possess," she insists, but there is only one surefire way to find out if you can be successful: "Just give it a try."

3. *Making Work Work for the Highly Sensitive Person: Learning to Bend, Not Break When Work Overwhelms You* by Barrie S. Jaeger. In spite of the clunky title (who sees herself as *insensitive*?), this book from a "work therapist" creates three categories for thinking about your career. Drudgery: It pays the rent. Craft: It hones your skills. Calling: It fulfills your dreams and talents. Don't have a clue what your dream job might be? Write two pages summing up your life as a fairy tale. "Grow yourself," says Jaeger, "and your real work will grow toward you."

4. *Bonjour Laziness: Why Hard Work Doesn't Pay* by Corinne Maier. Psychoanalyst Maier is anything but the organization man. The corporate world "has no use for noble passions," she says in this mocking prescription for surviving it by laying low. Is she serious? Well, yes and no. The real aim of this amusing take on "corporate culture" ("Culture, my ass!") is its hypocrisy. "The more big business talks about something, the less of it there is," Maier writes. Ergo, beware any company that says it "values" its employees or the manager who says, "I practice consensus politics."

5. *One Tough Mother: Success in Life, Business and Apple Pies* by Gert Boyle with Kerry Tymchuk. After a heart attack killed her husband in 1970, Boyle watched as their small outdoor-apparel company teetered on collapse. Now she's famous as "Chairman Ma," centerfold for the ad campaign promoting what has become a megacompany, Columbia Sportswear. "Ask me to swim a mile and I'd say, 'No way,'" she says. "But if someone took me out on a boat and pushed me into the ocean a mile from shore, you better believe I would start swimming." We believe it.

6. *Lipstick Jungle* by Candace Bushnell. This look at the more glamorous side of the Manhattan work world features three powerful pals, slightly older than the men-seeking quartet in Bushnell's *Sex in the City*. Magazine honcho Nico wears red minks to match her hair and treats her lover like a sex object. Movie mogul Wendy supports her metrosexual husband's spending sprees while an English nanny (the accent costs "an extra $50,000") raises their kids. Fashion designer Victory dates a sexist billionaire. They are as ruthless as men. But, as this cautionary tale of ambition shows, power has its down side—no matter which sex is holding the reins.

7. *The Prize Winner of Defiance, Ohio: How My Mother Raised 10 Kids in 25 Words or Less* by Terry Ryan. During the 1950s and '60s, Evelyn Ryan earned her living at the kitchen table, writing jingles for the likes of Burma-Shave and the *Bob Hope Show*. Daughter Terry recaptures the times, her father's drinking problem, and her mother's forbearance, wrapping them all in the manna of contest entries that yielded cash, toys, appliances, and even two cars. To her children, the bounty seemed so miraculous that "we began to suspect she had a direct line to God."

8. *A Broom of One's Own* by Nancy Peacock. After publishing two novels, Peacock still had to work as a housecleaner to make ends meet. Was she a writer or a maid? In these hilarious essays, she contemplates her two "brilliant careers," providing sharp insight into both. Her reluctance to stop cleaning other people's toilets (she finally does hang up the mop) may not have been entirely financial. "I think there are two things writers love more than anything else. One is solitude and the other is gossip. In the housecleaning trade, I got both."

9. *Treatment Kind and Fair: Letters to a Young Doctor* by Perri Klass. Noting that medicine "is not a reflective profession," pediatrician and veteran writer Klass proceeds to make it one in these letters to her med school–bound son, Orlando. Assessing the education and rituals that shape an M.D., she also delivers a manifesto for patients' rights, stressing the responsibility that goes with invading other peoples' lives "at the moments of highest drama and sharpest anxiety and deepest sorrow." Her compassion should guide anyone in medicine or any helping profession.

10. *Why Women Should Rule the World* by Dee Dee Myers. As the first woman White House press secretary, Myers had a smaller office, a lower salary, and less access than her predecessors: "responsibility without corresponding authority," a predicament women know well, she says, in this rumination on women and power. Isolated examples (like Margaret Thatcher) won't change the world, she argues. What's needed are more women at the table. In the boardroom, the magic number seems to be three. Only then do the dynamics change: "Suddenly, women are no longer seen as outsiders."

TO TAKE TO YOUR INVESTMENT CLUB

1. *Money, a Memoir: Women, Emotions and Cash* by Liz Perle. Perle never thought much about money until after her marriage collapsed, when she found she had none. She combines sociological inquiry and personal tell-all to gauge women's attitudes toward money and speak candidly of her own feelings about what is too often a taboo subject for women. Her warning: "As long as we let emotions influence—even dictate—our financial lives, we remain prey to unhealthy, at times destructive relationships."

2. *Prince Charming Isn't Coming: How Women Get Smart About Money* by Barbara Stanny. Born with a silver spoon, Stanny entrusted that spoon to a husband who squandered much of it. So, postdivorce, she became an early evangelist for women as their own money managers. Stanny's pep talk, first published a decade ago, argues that controlling your own money gives you power, so don't leave the decisions to some guy, even your spouse. She demystifies investing and preaches caution: Start small, diversify, know what you're buying, and learn from your mistakes (men make them, too).

3. *Not Buying It: My Year Without Shopping* by Judith Levine. Levine was disgusted with consumerism—her own. So, for a year, she and her husband made a pact: Give up luxuries and buy only necessities (groceries, toilet paper, Internet access, cat medicine). The result? She missed movies; he missed Q-tips. Their savings went up and their fights about money vanished. But, more importantly, says Levine in this account of their year of deprivation, they became better citizens: "Self-exiled from the shops and eateries, we had no place to hang out but the olde publick square."

4. *Shopaholic and Baby* by Sophie Kinsella. To Becky Brandon, not buying is akin to not breathing. In this fifth installment of Kinsella's hilarious shopaholic series, Becky is a mother-to-be who has to learn about a whole new market aimed at mothers-to-be, from Baby Einstein to the Circus Tent Changing Station. The series is, of course, a spoof on today's label-demented society and its search for meaning through acquisition. But who's judging? This time, Becky has her priorities straight: "It's all about the baby"—dressed, of course, in a "gorgeous little white Dior babygro."

5. *Bait and Switch: The (Futile) Pursuit of the American Dream* by Barbara Ehrenreich. You earn a college degree, play by the rules, do everything right. And still end up in ruin. This is the bait and switch Ehrenreich warns about in this reportage on the middle-class job market. After working low-paying jobs for a year (see *Nickel and Dimed*), Ehrenreich thought a year undercover as a middle-class job seeker would be a piece of cake. She was wrong. "White-collar unemployment—and the poverty that often results—remains a rude finger in the face of the American dream."

6. *The Logic of Life: The Rational Economics of an Irrational World* by Tim Harford. If you liked the best seller *Freakonomics,* this one's for you. Harford, a member of the *Financial Times* editorial board, believes that rationality not only controls checkbooks but also factors into decisions people make about love, sex, and office politics. To wit: Fear of AIDS leads to more oral sex. If you buy his line, rational behavior doesn't produce a perfect world, but at least it's more predictable. And predictability is music to the ears of any economist.

7. *Moral Hazard* by Kate Jennings. For a fictional view of Wall Street and the investment world, try this smart novel narrated by a woman who writes speeches for the titans of finance. Her husband has Alzheimer's, and she needs the paycheck to pay for his treatment. So, "commuting, it seemed, between two forms of dementia," Cath befriends the head of her firm's risk-management unit, who disabuses her of any notion that risk can be managed. Do tell: Coping with her mate's decline and a hedge fund meltdown, Cath takes you behind the curtain of a cutthroat world.

8. *Dynasties: Fortunes & Misfortunes of the World's Great Family Businesses* by David S. Landes. Putting high finance in personal terms, this user-friendly read shows how the Rothschilds emerged from Frankfurt's Jewish ghetto and how the Rockefellers built their legacy on oil and one notoriously difficult man. In search of the winning formula among various dynastic empires, Landes uncovers shrewdness, of course, but also luck, dedication, and flexibility. The family behind the Toyota car empire sums up its forward vision in a one-word motivational slogan, *kaizen.* Translation: never good enough.

9. *The Number: What Do You Need for the Rest of Your Life and What Will It Cost* by Lee Eisenberg. You know your Number— the amount of moola you think you need for retirement—but how good are your calculations? In this provocative book, Eisenberg examines the pitfalls of financial planning. Many advisors are deaf and dumb to what it takes to "make your heart sing through old age," he says. "A financial plan without a meaning plan leads straight to the thudding realization that—duh—all the money in the world doesn't buy happiness."

10. *American Sucker* by David Denby. Irrational exuberance seized Denby as his marriage tanked in 1999. Enchanted by the New Economy—fiber optics! biotech!—the writer and critic chased after it as a way to offset the cost of divorce. Here he soul-searches about the stock market's surge and fall, how much he lost, and what separates healthy acquisitiveness from greed. Denby ends up less bitter than philosophical about his losses: "I acted as if money were an end in itself," he writes. "I threw myself into the new religion, and I forgot all the ways it could fool you."

THAT FACE ILLNESS STRAIGHT ON

1. *Anatomy of an Illness as Perceived by the Patient* by Norman Cousins. This classic, first published in 1979, comes from a man whose writing about medicine led the focus on the mind-body connection. After being told that he had an incurable disease, Cousins fought back with belly laughs and vitamin C. But forget the crystals: He endorses judicious use of conventional therapies, good nutrition, and big doses of your own positive energy when the body goes on strike. "We gorge the senses and starve the sensibilities," he writes. What's amazing is not how sick you can get, but how resilient your body can be.

2. *Nordie's at Noon: The Personal Stories of Four Women "Too Young" for Breast Cancer* by Patti Balwanz, Kim Carlos, Jennifer Johnson, and Jana Peters. Four women, all diagnosed with breast cancer when they were thirty or younger, become "bosom buddies," meeting for mutual support at a Nordstrom café near their Kansas City homes. Here, they discuss treatment choices, family reactions, the role of faith, and attitude toward death. (Patti's family finished her portion when she lost her battle at age twenty-nine.) One thing they all agreed on: No one is "too young" for breast cancer.

3. *Cancer Vixen* by Marisa Acocella Marchetto. "What happens when a shoe-crazy, lipstick-obsessed, wine-swilling, pasta-slurping, fashion-fanatic, single-forever, about-to-get-married, big-city girl cartoonist with a fabulous life finds . . . a lump in her breast?" asks this brassy New Yorker in a memoir drawn in bold, primary colors. Well, she doesn't call off her wedding to famed restaurant owner Silvano Marchetto. No, with the support of friends, a bossy mother, and her down-to-earth fiancé, and after "29 needles, 18 pounds, 15 radiation technicians, 11 medical assistants, 9 nurses, 8 doctors, $192,720.04, 2 rabbis and 1 priest," she faces down the Big C.

4. *Lying Awake* by Mark Salzman. This novel is about illness, physical and spiritual. A neurologist tells Sister John, a Carmelite nun, that her mystical visions are not coming from God but from a tumor. An operation would stop her seizures, but would it return her to a spiritual desert? Salzman refuses to provide easy answers for either Sister John or his readers: "Is God asking me to let go of concerns for my health, or is he asking me to let go of my desire for his presence?" asks Sister John. Can you walk in faith, despite your doubts?

5. *The Book of Dahlia* by Elisa Albert. When twenty-nine-year-old Dahlia Finger is diagnosed with a terminal brain tumor, her shallow mind "vacillates between feeling furious that her fate was gossip fodder and feeling furious at the possibility that there wasn't *even* gossip swirling about her." She's a gal with a 'tude, and no chemo or radiation treatments or pitying glances or smarmy poetry can take that away from her. This novel is less about disease of the body than afflictions of the soul and contemporary life as Dahlia takes ironic appraisal of past and present. *Seinfeld* fans, unite.

6. *The Family That Couldn't Sleep: A Medical Mystery* by D. T. Max. For centuries, members of an Italian noble family have been struck down at random by a fierce and fatal insomnia. What causes this curse? Deadly misfolded proteins called prions, says science writer Max, whose reportage on these terrifying invaders reads like a detective story. For him, it's personal: He, too, suffers from a genetic neurological disease. And when he gets to the part about how prions are also linked to less rare diseases such as mad cow and Alzheimer's, you'll be calling for more research, too.

7. *Refuge: An Unnatural History of Family and Place* by Terry Tempest Williams. "Genealogy is in our blood," Williams, a Mormon from pioneer stock, writes. "As a people and a family, we have a sense of history." These twin ideas echo through a book that deals alternately with the natural landscape and her mother's slow dying. Tracking bird life in the Great Salt Lake Basin, Williams suspects exposure to atomic bomb testing in the '50s may account for the legacy of female cancers she inherited. Meanwhile, she writes, "An individual doesn't get cancer, a family does."

8. *Veronica* by Mary Gaitskill. Alison, a washed-up ex-model with hepatitis C, is the central character in this sorrowful novel. So who's Veronica, the title character? By pointing to Alison's caustic, ugly friend, who died from AIDS, Gaitskill shows how illness can create insight and, often, regrets. "She wanted to be a victim," Alison reflects. "She'd made choices." Yet now that she's sick and alone, the once-beautiful Alison questions her cavalier regard for a friend who in the end had no one else. It turns out that the two women had more in common than she'd ever thought.

9. *The Noonday Demon: An Atlas of Depression* by Andrew Solomon. Prozac can't solve everything, Solomon says, describing depression as one part body chemistry, one part emotional set point that a blood test can't measure. Still, in this blend of personal experience and careful research, he eloquently describes how it feels (for him and others), available treatments, and the slowly evolving acceptance of the disease. "The greatest block to progress is still probably social stigma," Solomon writes—a claim that makes this candid, intelligent work all the more valuable.

10. *Learning to Fall: The Blessings of an Imperfect Life* by Philip Simmons. Simmons's metaphor for learning how to live well in the face of great loss—learning to fall—was not just a figure of speech. At thirty-five, married with two children, he was diagnosed with ALS, a degenerative disease that caused him serious physical tumbles. Now after his death, these lyrical meditations remain as a reminder not of loss but what, despite his illness, remained: family, nature, imagination. "In the act of letting go of our lives, we return more fully to them."

FOR TAKING ON CARETAKING

1. *The Afterlife: Memoir of a Mother's Madness* by Donald Antrim. "The anxious child of a childlike mother," novelist Antrim was an early caretaker, acting as a substitute husband for an alcoholic, self-destructive mother. In these essays, prompted by his mother's death, he tries to come to terms with this cruel role reversal. The mundane act of buying a new bed, the recollection of an outlandish kimono she created—everything reveals her continued hold on him. "I could not imagine life without my mother. And it was true as well that only without her would I feel able to live."

2. *A Heartbreaking Work of Staggering Genius* by Dave Eggers. "You like that stance, that underdog stance," accuses a friend in this almost-true story about a young guy struggling to hold life and family together after both parents drop dead of cancer. At twenty-two, Eggers becomes the horny and confused father substitute for his nine-year-old brother, even as both are seen as "celebrity orphans" at Toph's school. The self-deprecating Eggers owns up to changes in his account that were made for dramatic effect, but those are details: Concerning the emotional truths, he doesn't miss a beat.

3. *A Short History of Tractors in Ukrainian* by Marina Lewycka. A widowed eighty-four-year-old has fallen for a thirty-six-year-old blonde with big boobs from his native Ukraine in this novel about family caretaking. Although his two daughters have been feuding over their mother's inheritance, they unite in opposing this improbable union, believing that the "tart" is only after their father's pension. You'll laugh and cry, sometimes on the same page, while learning a lot about tractors, Ukrainian history, and the difficulties in understanding what your parents need as they age.

4. *Where Is the Mango Princess?* by Cathy Crimmins. "You just love me for my brain," Crimmins's husband, Al, used to joke when they were in grad school. Now he delivers the line with a bitter edge, after surviving a boating accident with a permanent head injury. His change "sometimes leaves me so weak with anguish I can barely get out of bed," Crimmins writes. Yet somehow she does, and ferociously so. The resident who wrote "wife uncooperative" on Al's chart needed a lesson medical schools don't teach: to what lengths a reasonable woman will go for someone she loves.

5. *Two Weeks to Live: A Memoir of Love, Death and Politics* by Eleanor Clift. Here, journalist Clift intersperses two cases of caretaking, one very private—at home with her husband and writing partner, Tom Brazaitis, dying of cancer; the other grotesquely public—the headline-grabbing story of Terri Schiavo and the fight over whether to take her off a feeding tube. Clift draws an important lesson from both deaths (they died within days of each other): "This aspect of life, the dying part, will happen to all of us, and it's time that we get acquainted with how you do it."

6. *Janet & Me: An Illustrated Story of Love and Loss* by Stan Mack. With humor and honesty, cartoonist Mack describes how he cared for his stubborn and energetic companion of eighteen years, Janet Bode, who died of breast cancer. The most poignant moments are visual, but his words will knock you out cold (chapter 10: "The Joke's Over. You Can Come Back Now"). The hardest part? Accepting help: "When friends first brought food over, my first thought was, our friends are talking about us. And I was offended. Don't they think I can take care of Janet?"

7. *The Crazed* by Ha Jin. In this novel about political correctness, Chinese-style, aspiring scholar Jian Wan is assigned to care for the brain-damaged professor who is both his mentor and father of his fiancé. Given his nickname as "the Poet," it's no surprise that Jian is all thumbs as a caregiver. But his bigger flaw is his passiveness, which is gradually transformed as he listens to the patient, whose injured mind offers unfiltered truths that change the course of Jian's life.

8. *Dancing with Rose: Finding Life in the Land of Alzheimer's* by Lauren Kessler. "There is a way of looking at Alzheimer's that is not about decline and loss but is instead about movement from the worldly to the spiritual," Kessler writes after months spent working as an aide in a "memory care" facility. A journalism professor and writer, she took the job to confront her experience caring for her own mother, who succumbed to the disease. Her window on the Alzheimer's world gives perspective and empathy for its sufferers, showing that wit and personality abide even as memory fails.

9. *Another Country: Navigating the Emotional Terrain of Our Elders* by Mary Pipher. Trying to understand the world old people inhabit, Pipher comes up with astute observations about how aging changes the parent-child relationship. She notes that what separates Baby Boomers from the previous generations is less digital technology than psychology, because older people were taught to suppress their pain. What links everyone—and contributes to America's "social sickness"—is the emphasis on independence, Pipher writes. "We have no language for nurturing interdependency."

10. *An Uncertain Inheritance: Writers on Caring for Family* edited by Nell Casey. Ann Harleman remembers her "other husband," the one without MS. Helen Shulman and her brother, spent by their father's long illness, "plot" to kill him. Eleanor Cooney likens herself to the last man of a doomed expedition, writing his diary "right up to the bitter end." These caretakers and others in this anthology describe vividly and, yes, often with humor, life within "the black balloon." Don't see them as heroes. As Stephen Yadzinski says: "Anyone would have done what I did."

FOR THE GRIEVING HEART

1. *A Grief Observed* by C. S. Lewis. British scholar and avowed Christian Lewis married late, only to see his wife die four years later of cancer. Here he writes about the sorrow and crisis of faith that followed her death. "The time when there is nothing at all in your soul except a cry for help may be just the time when God can't give it," he realizes. Grief numbs the response to God and to the world, but not permanently. His heartfelt summary of the passage from despair to reconciliation offers a hopeful message to anyone coping with the loss of someone she loves.

2. *Elegy* by Mary Jo Bang. "I say Come Back and you do / Not do what I want. / The train unrolls its track and sends its sound forward." As poet Bang describes the year after her grown son died, details are sketchy, but words like *young* and *sudden* and *suicide* dwell beneath pain that is seldom so honestly and bravely portrayed. You see a world irrevocably split between when he was here and now that he's gone, and even though a sense of betrayal lingers at the edges, what's first and foremost is the "Grief of the mother / Whose child has been swept away."

3. *Grief* by Andrew Holleran. In this novel, a professor who has been his mother's primary caretaker in Florida moves to Washington, D.C., after her death. Meeting up with fellow gays still reeling from the AIDS epidemic and struggling with survivor's guilt, he isolates himself, reading the letters of another griever, Mary Todd Lincoln. But whether grieving for friends or family, everyone has a need for ongoing intimacy. As his friend, Frank, reminds him, "When your parents die, you know, your audience is gone . . . But I think somebody has to care about you—someone has to think you matter."

4. *About Alice* by Calvin Trillin. When Alice Trillin died of a heart attack on September 11, 2001, of all days, Trillin received a surprising number of condolences from strangers. People, he says, felt like they knew the wife he portrayed in his books with such obvious affection (as in *Alice, Let's Eat*). In this spare tribute, he wants to set the record straight and reveal the "real" Alice. Written from the ground zero of his grief, it only serves to reinforce the sentiments of one of those consolers: a young woman who wrote that she sometimes looks at her boyfriend and asks, "But will he love me like Calvin loves Alice?"

5. *The Sea* by John Banville. In this winner of England's most prestigious literary prize, the Man Booker, the newly widowed Max Morden returns to the seaside town where he first witnessed death. Then and now blend as the fictional Max offers a soliloquy on life and loss, both seen through the glass darkly. *"Do not look so worried,* Anna said, *I hated you, too, a little, we were human beings, after all.* Yet for all that, I cannot rid myself of the conviction that we missed something, that I missed something, only I do not know what it might have been."

6. *The Year of Magical Thinking* by Joan Didion. Didion offers a startlingly honest account of her reaction to her husband and fellow writer John Gregory Dunne's sudden death by heart attack while they are trying to cope with the illness of their only child, Quintana. Written from the notes she took during the year after her husband's death, this memoir is an amazing look at the craziness of grief and the depths of denial we all feel toward

POST SCRIPTS:
TURNING GRIEF INTO MEMORIES

When my mom died at age ninety-two, my three sisters and I gathered her writings into a book. *Post Scripts: A Writing Life After Eighty* by LaVerne Hammond was published through BookSurge, an arm of amazon.com.

It was a healing experience.

The book is a tribute to our mother, but it is also a reminder to everyone that it is never too late to realize your dreams. LaVerne always had wanted to be a writer, but marriage and children derailed her ambitions. Then, at eighty-six, she sold an article about a touching experience she had at a yard sale to the *St. Petersburg Times*. That article led to a late-blooming career as a monthly columnist for the newspaper's new Seniority section. By age ninety-two, her byline had appeared over more than seventy published pieces, including "A Letter to Lara," addressed to her recently born first great-grandchild, written in the hospital shortly before she died.

Our mom's late-in-life career grew out of a project that she launched just after our dad died: She began writing down the story of her life. Sometimes she wrote a letter to someone important in her life, both the living and the dead: her father, her grandmother, or an old boyfriend. Other times, she simply recorded a funny or touching anecdote she thought her family would enjoy. When she died, among her possessions, we found a box of these gems marked Memoirs.

We also found dozens of books with such titles as *One Memory at a Time: Inspiration & Advice for Writing Your Family Story*; *To Our Children's Children: Preserving Family Histories for Generations to Come*; *Homemade Biography: How to Collect, Record, and Tell the*

Life Story of Someone You Love; and *Turning Memories into Memoirs: A Handbook for Writing Life Stories.*

One book, *Leaving a Trace: The Art of Transforming a Life Into Stories,* by Alexandra Johnson, was opened to chapter 6 and a quote by Toni Morrison:

"Gaining access to that interior life is a kind of . . . archaeology: On the basis of some information and a little bit of guesswork you journey to a site to see what remains were left behind and you reconstruct the world."

~ Margo

---

the subject of death. "Grief, when it comes, is nothing like we expect it to be."

7. *ABC: A Novel* by David Plante. A similar confusion and displacement of grief haunts the protagonist in this novel, which starts with a terrible accident that leaves a young couple bereft. Gerard, the father, found a note written in Sanskrit moments before his son's tragic death occurred, and in the months following, he becomes obsessed with the order of the alphabet. His seemingly esoteric quest is really a struggle to make sense of losing his child: "What was the vast longing of the dead that only the living could try to fulfill for them, but always fail to fulfill? What was it?"

8. *The Lovely Bones* by Alice Sebold. The brutal murder of a fourteen-year-old who then tells her story from her perch in the

afterworld are the distinguishing marks of this popular novel. But not to be missed is the true-to-life arc Sebold creates for the victim's family, which is spun apart by grief but slowly comes together as time passes. The "lovely bones" of the title have nothing to do with her remains and everything to do with what connects the survivors, who must go forward with their focus on each other rather than the teenager torn from their midst.

9. *Will the Circle Be Unbroken? Reflections on Death, Rebirth, and Hunger for a Faith* by Studs Terkel. Terkel's books are like therapy sessions: honest thoughts from real people. Here, he interviews a woman who had been in a two-year coma, an innocent man who spent years on death row, AIDS and breast cancer survivors, a police officer, a firefighter, a hoodlum, medics, believers, and atheists about their views on death. A downer? Not at all. These monologues are surprisingly life affirming. This book is "about death but it's really about how we live that prelude to death, life."

10. *The Little Prince* by Antoine de Saint Exupery. Written and whimsically illustrated by a French pilot who flew reconnaissance missions during World War II, this strange tale is about a pilot who meets a tiny prince after his airplane is downed over the Sahara Desert. It's not about death per se, but rather about those things that transcend death: love, for example. Often mistakenly classified as a children's story, the message really is for adults who have lost hope, something children rarely do. Eerily, the author's plane disappeared over the Mediterranean one year after *The Little Prince* was published.

THAT TAKE THE DIS OUT OF DISABILITIES

1. *The Voice: A Memoir* by Thomas Quasthoff. Barely four feet tall and left armless by Thalidomide, Quasthoff tells funny and mind-boggling stories in this memoir about how his parents fought to raise him as an equal. Now a world-class baritone with three Grammys, he prefers to talk about Bach and jazz, not his disability. "I'm not a role model," he says, pointing to lingering discrimination against the physically incapacitated. "Less spectacularly disabled people still have a hard time finding employment." He wants your respect, not your pity: "Sympathy is free, but envy must be earned."

2. *In the Shadow of Memory* by Floyd Skloot. "I used to be able to think," this former marathon runner starts out, recalling the astute and agile person he left behind before a virus carved lesions on his brain. The result: At age forty-one, he couldn't remember how to tie his shoes, much less recall the words needed to pursue a writer's vocation. "Static dementia," the docs called it. But here's perfect evidence that Skloot never stood still in the effort to overcome his illness. "I began to realize that the most aggressive act I could perform on my own behalf was to stop struggling and discover what I could really do."

3. *Talk, Talk* by T. C. Boyle. This novel about identity theft will send you to the paper shredder. Dana Halter, a deaf woman, discovers someone is using her name when she's mistakenly arrested and spends a traumatic weekend in jail. She becomes determined to track down the thief who stole her life. As a relentless chase takes her and her hearing boyfriend cross-country, testing the limits of their love, Boyle conjures Halter's proud world of finger-spelling: *"When deaf get together talk talk all the time.* Communication, the universal need. Information. Access. Escape from the prison of silence."

4. *Deafening* by Frances Itani. In another novel that evokes the world of the deaf, love and war are wrapped around the story of Grania O'Neill, who loses her hearing after a childhood bout with scarlet fever. Growing up in Ontario at the turn of the twentieth century, she learns to read lips and sign with the help of her grandmother and the deaf school. Yet what fascinates most is Itani's depiction of her thoughts. When her beloved tries to share what he hears in the wind, she nods, not bothering to explain that her interior life already resonates with silent music. "Sound was always more important to the hearing."

5. *Epileptic* by David B. This autobiographical graphic novel portrays the author's growing up in France during the 1960s and '70s. When his older brother, Jean-Christophe, began having seizures, the whole family was affected, both by his brother's rage over his illness and his parents' efforts (both conventional and bizarre) to get treatment and cure him. Pierre-Francois, a.k.a. David B., escapes through fantasy games and dreams. This is a haunting look not just at epilepsy but also at the family as a body in which one ailing part can play havoc with the rest.

6. *Secret Girl* by Molly Bruce Jacobs. "It may be the first real thing you've ever done," Jacobs's doctor says about her decision, at age thirty-eight, to meet her retarded sister, Anne. Institutionalized since birth, Anne had been a family secret, one that haunted Jacobs and grieved her parents, who coped by putting a tourniquet on their emotions. After a divorce and rehab for a drinking problem, she tracks down her sister and becomes her friend. This bittersweet memoir blends compassion with the reality of choices made long ago.

7. *Poster Child* by Emily Rapp. Body image takes on a whole new meaning in Rapp's account of being born with a deformity that led to the loss of her leg and repeated operations. Being chosen poster child for the March of Dimes was small compensation, she recalls: "I hated my body. I prayed for a new one." The road to self-acceptance has been slow, with detours like anorexia showing how hard it was. But in Rapp's story you witness the value of a loving family, her own strength of character, and advances in prosthetics that have vastly improved an amputee's quality of life.

8. *Little Beauties* by Kim Addonizio. In this novel by poet Addonizio, thirty-four-year-old Diana McBride struggles with an obsessive-compulsive disorder: "I am the Princess of Soapsuds. The Lather Queen." Her OCD has driven her husband away. She hates her haircut. And her alcoholic mother keeps calling. No wonder she needs to wash herself constantly. She works at a baby shop, the most sanitized place she could find, but when she lets a seventeen-year-old unwed mother and her newborn into her life, she must rein in her obsession with perfection. Love comes with a whole lot of messiness.

9. *Motherless Brooklyn* by Jonathan Lethem. This is a detective novel. But the language-shattering expletives that erupt from its narrator are the antithesis of the genre's usual cool dick. Lionel Essrog has Tourette's syndrome. (In his "echo-chamber skull," his name comes out Liable Gusscog or Final Escow.) But as Lethem delightfully demonstrates, Essrog's tics and manic language blend in perfectly with his chaotic surroundings. New York is a "Tourettic city," from the "great communal scratching and counting and tearing" of its lottery ticket buyers to its subway walls layered, like Essrog's brain, "with expulsive and incoherent language."

10. *A Healing Family* by Kenzaburo Oe. Oe's son, born with a brain abnormality, has a limited ability to communicate. At least, with words. The irony is not lost on his father, who won the 1994 Nobel Prize for Literature. Here, he describes the joys, angers, and sorrows of life with Hikari, and how he and his wife have encouraged him to compose music, "the only means by which we can fully understand his emotions." Says Oe, whose novel *A Personal Matter* was about a parent with a brain-damaged son: "I feel in awe of the richness of his inner life."

THAT VISIT SORROW'S KITCHEN

1. *The Collected Autobiographies of Maya Angelou* by Maya Angelou. "What you looking at me for / I didn't come to stay" is the first line of "I Know Why the Caged Bird Sings," Angelou's powerful account of her early years. It's also the final line in "A Song Flung Up to Heaven," the last volume of her six autobiographies, which are anthologized here. The line "seems to say however low you perceive me now, I am headed for higher ground," says Angelou. It's a perfect way to bookend stories about a triumphant life that started out so troubled.

2. *Stuart: A Life Backwards* by Alexander Masters. It is Stuart Shorter who suggests that his story be told backwards, time-traveling through alcoholic hazes to his sad childhood, to find out "what murdered the boy I was." Masters, an American social worker in London, obliges, but he finds no easy answers about why people like Stuart end up on the streets. His honest and truly funny portrait of his knife-wielding friend, one of the "chaotic homeless," is guaranteed to haunt you. Who would have thought such a genuine friendship was possible between a have and have-not?

3. *The God of War* by Marisa Silver. Twelve-year-old Ares Ramirez lives in the California desert with his single working mom, Laurel, and brain-damaged brother, Malcolm. In her quest for independence, Laurel is as untethered to the world around her as the trailer they call home. No surprise, then, that she brushes off signs that both Malcolm and Ares are headed toward trouble. "No one can tell me they know my boys better than I do," she says. When violence erupts, it seems preordained, proving that if love isn't anchored to reality, people can get hurt.

4. *The Things Between Us: A Memoir* by Lee Montgomery. Montgomery's story opens with her dad mixing her mother's first cocktail of the day—at 8:45 A.M. You can imagine the drunken spells and blackouts that go from there. Growing up in a family that deflected her mom's drinking problem with dark humor and willed ignorance, Montgomery takes on the issue when her "eternally bemused" father is dying from cancer. "You could have gotten away with offing Mom without being fried," she tells him. "I blew it," he admits. Instead of murder, an intervention would have been nice.

5. *When Katie Wakes: A Memoir* by Connie May Fowler. Fowler's novel about child abuse, *When Women Had Wings,* made into a TV movie starring Oprah Winfrey, wasn't completely fictional. In this memoir, Fowler describes fleeing her own mother's beatings, only to take up with a man who put cigarettes out on her face. She finally breaks away, with help from her dog, Katie. But not before a suicide attempt: "I set the oven to three-fifty. If it's good enough for a casserole, it ought to be good enough for me." As she confirms, abuse leaves more than just physical scars.

6. *Property* by Valerie Martin. This novel set in the antebellum South shows how the subjugated turn on those weaker rather than challenge their subjugators. The childless Manon, lady of the manor, hates her husband but turns her hostility on Sarah, the black slave who has borne her husband's offspring. This erotically charged look at the hierarchy of plantation life shows masters tense and slaves restive under the whip. After Sarah tries to escape by masquerading as a white man, Manon tells her aunt, "She has tasted a freedom you and I will never know."

7. *The Baby Thief: The Untold Story of Georgia Tann, the Baby Seller Who Corrupted Adoption* by Barbara Bisantz Raymond. "Young women in trouble, call Miss Georgia Tann." Lured by this newspaper ad, unwed moms were drawn into a Memphis adoption mill that, starting in the 1920s, even used kidnapping to maintain a steady flow of adoptable infants for "high type" families. Tann preyed on the poor and powerless, regarding them as "trashy people." For Raymond, an adoptive mother, Tann's legacy offers an extreme example of a system that put children's interests last.

8. *Heart Like Water: Surviving Katrina and Life in Its Disaster Zone* by Joshua Clark. At first, sitting out the hurricane was an adventure: In its wake, Clark and his girlfriend strolled the French Quarter in bathrobes and flip-flops, as if on holiday. But then came the flooding and its shocking results. Clark roamed the city, recording the breakdown with his Radio Shack tape recorder. Noting that the destruction of the wetlands set the stage, he writes, "Mississippi suffered the storm's violence, while Louisiana suffered man's negligence, and therein lies the greater tragedy."

9. *Princess Sultana's Daughters* by Jean Sasson. Even the privilege of royalty doesn't protect females in a male-dominated world, according to this sad account of life behind the veil. Told to Sasson by "Princess Sultana," the pen name of a royal Saudi family member, this second book in a trilogy tells of rapes, forced marriage, and the hardship of raising girls in a country that imposes such an "unbearable restrictive lifestyle" on women. One daughter already has had a mental breakdown. "How lamentable . . . so much ignorance should prevail in a land that is home to a great religion."

10. *A Piece of Cake* by Cupcake Brown. When Cupcake Brown's Momma died, she thought her life was hell. "Little did I know, my hell hadn't even begun," says Brown in this searing memoir about her life on Philadelphia's mean streets. She also didn't know how resilient she was. Managing to survive sadistic foster parents, rape, gangbanging, prostitution, homelessness, and an addiction to crack cocaine, she is now a lawyer and inspirational speaker. "I have completely forgiven everyone who's ever hurt, harmed, failed, or doubted me, starting with—*and especially*—me."

THAT CROSS CULTURES

1. *Fasting, Feasting* by Anita Desai. Desai, mother of Kiran (see number 2), tackles not only the generational divide but also the chasm between India and the United States in this bifurcated novel. It starts in India with adult daughter Uma and her claustrophobic role as caretaker for Mama and Papa. It moves to America, where only son Arun carries the weight of their expectations to college. His summer break in the 'burbs includes a clueless host mom ("India—gee!"), a bulimic daughter, and the sense that family dynamics are weird everywhere. It's a small world, after all.

2. *The Inheritance of Loss* by Kiran Desai. Desai, daughter of Anita (see number 1), shows off her own formidable skills as a novelist in a story that casts the lens wide. Retired Indian judge Jemubhai Patel and his granddaughter, Sai, live a quiet life in the Himalayas until conflict and the effects of a global economy knock at their door. The prose is both lyrical and energetic, using snippets of dialect, as a romance falls under the wheels of ethnic tensions, the green card turns out to be a lousy one to draw, and—as usual—the powerless are the biggest losers.

3. *Mixed: My Life in Black and White* by Angela Nissel. "Being a mixed child, you get used to people staring at you," says Nissel in this memoir that offers its own mix of humor and pathos. Estranged from a philandering white father and raised by a former Black Panther, Nissel endured whites calling her a "zebra" and blacks telling her she wasn't black enough. In college, the confusion sent her to a psych ward. Now, married to a man whose "family photos look like the covers of World History textbooks," she just laughs at "how surreal being biracial in America can be."

4. *American Woman* by Susan Choi. Homegrown subcultures can be as alien as any. Here, the radical underground meets conventional America in a fictionalized twist on the Patty Hearst story. It's the mid-'70s, and former bomb-thrower Jenny Shimada is lying low under an assumed name. When she's asked to give refuge to a trio of fellow radicals, including the kidnapped "Princess," she learns that terrorists are not your usual house-guests (the guns were a tip-off). Choi captures the bizarre mind-set of those "who thought they could make history, while all the while *it* had made *them.*"

5. *The Garden of Last Days* by Andre Dubus III. The route to 9/11 starts at a stripper's club in this dark meeting of American tawdriness and Islamic fundamentalism. April, a.k.a. exotic dancer Spring, takes her three-year-old daughter to the club when her usual babysitter is sick. Bassam prepares for jihad by getting close and personal with the "stupid people living to please Shay-tan (Satan) and not even knowing it." Peering into these low-lit corners, you'll see how different the world looks to a lonely man holding a drink and some twenties and a naked woman who needs his money.

6. *Lipstick Jihad: A Memoir of Growing Up Iranian in America and American in Iran* by Azadeh Moaveni. Graphic artist Marjane Satrapi's *Persepolis* is set in Iran. Firoozeh Dumas's *Funny in Farsi* is set in America. This memoir is set in both countries. Moaveni was born into California's Iranian-American community and worked for *Time* magazine in Tehran. She looks at her two homes with a hard journalist's eye, letting neither off the hook. Today's Iran is "spiritually and psychologically wrecked," she writes. But in America, "I could die from food poisoning from takeout, and no one would find me for days."

7. *Come on Shore and We Will Kill and Eat You All: A New Zealand Story* by Christina Thompson. Thompson, an American scholar of the Pacific, artfully blends her personal story with the history of New Zealand's Maoris. Her own "first contact" with that indigenous people resulted in her marriage to a Maori named Seven, with whom she's had three children. The first encounters between European settlers and Maoris were far less congenial. "In each of you is a little bit of the conqueror and the conquered," she tells her boys, "the colonizer and the colonized."

8. *A Distant Shore* by Caryl Phillips. In a fictional story told from alternate points of view, mutual isolation plants the seeds of an unlikely friendship between a retired white schoolteacher and an immigrant handyman who is the only black person in her English subdivision. By training and temperament, Dorothy shouldn't befriend a "colored" guy. Likewise, Solomon has to ask to make sure he understands her: "You want me to come inside for tea?" Follow his lead and don't assume anything in this novel about the perils of cultural assimilation.

9. *Lives in Translation: Writers on Identity and Creativity* edited by Isabelle de Courtivron. Chile's Ariel Dorfman calls himself and other bilingual authors "wandering bigamists of language." Here, a French professor at MIT gathers essays by those two-tongued writers on what it's like "living in two languages, between two languages or in the overlap of two languages." For Ireland's Nuala Ni Dhomhnaill, bilingualism is a civic right: "My every act of writing, in Irish or English, is an attempt to alleviate what I think is a great loss and to promote a more inclusive, holistic attitude to the rich linguistic environment in which we all live."

10. *Digging to America* by Anne Tyler. This novel begins at the Baltimore airport where two families—one white American, the other Iranian-American—are picking up their adopted babies from Korea. Thanks to this chance encounter, the Donaldsons and the Yazdans form a friendship of sorts, marked by an Annual Party to celebrate their girls' arrival in America. With this premise, Tyler crafts a story of how culture shapes childhood, how the American melting pot works (and doesn't), and, in typical Tyler fashion, how the particular details of each individual family trumps everything.

VII

BABES IN THE
WORLD

Molly Ivins was an equal-opportunity basher. Although an unapologetic liberal, the satirist and syndicated columnist from Texas took aim at any politician she thought was too pompous or incompetent, from George W. Bush ("Shrub") to Bill Clinton ("weaker than bus-station chili").

As she put it, her job was to make "the ridiculous look ridiculous."

Ivins, who died of breast cancer in 2007, often urged her readers to take political action. "We are the deciders. . . . We need people in the streets, banging pots and pans and demanding, 'Stop it, now!'" she wrote of the Iraq war in her last column.

The authors of the books in this section don't goad readers to bang on pots and pans. They don't all share Ivins's views on the Iraq war. But they do reflect her feisty spirit and political skepticism, believing that democracy only works when people know what's up.

These books nudge you away from your day-to-day world and move you into a wider context. They open your eyes to the scary and thrilling developments of the twenty-first century: the dilemmas raised by technological and medical breakthroughs, the challenges of diversity and tolerance, and the issues surrounding the resurgence of religion. They urge you to learn about the environment, bone up on the history of women's progress, and ponder the issues of war and peace (and decide for yourself if you want to go out and bang those pots and pans).

And, yes, these books question authority.

Poking the powerful is a time-honored literary tradition in both nonfiction and fiction. Latin America has a long history of writers who mix social issues and literature. In *The Autumn of the Patriarch*, Nobel laureate Gabriel Garcia Marquez, master of magic realism, portrays a decaying dictator who symbolizes the danger of concentrated power. Argentinian Manuel Puig challenges his compatriots' machismo and homophobia in *Kiss of the Spider Woman*, the story of a political prisoner and homosexual who are thrown together in jail.

In this country, novelist Barbara Kingsolver has made social and economic justice the theme of her writing career, with books such as *The Bean Trees* (immigration), *The Poisonwood Bible* (colonialism in Africa), and *Pigs in Heaven* (cross-racial adoption). Writers take a chance when they weigh in on such controversial subjects. Kingsolver has to face down critics who call her work too political. Her retort: "If we can't, as artists, improve on real life, we should put down our pencils and go back to baking bread."

Taking a strong political stance is risky. In 1991, Susan Faludi won over women's rights activists when she criticized the antifeminist rants of Allan Bloom and Rush Limbaugh in *Backlash: The Undeclared War Against Women.* Nine years later, some of those fans took umbrage when she took a sympathetic look at working-class men in *Stiffed: The Betrayal of the Modern Man.*

Alienating readers is one thing; death threats are another. The fatwa against Salman Rushdie by Islamic fanatics pushed the Indian author into hiding for years, fearing for his life. In 2006, Russian journalist Anna Politkovskaya, author of *A Dirty War: A Russian Reporter in Chechnya,* was shot dead in an elevator in her Moscow apartment building. Her book, *Putin's Russia,* was never published in her native country but received the first English PEN Writers in Translation award.

For the late poet and short-story writer Grace Paley, the line between her writing life and her life work as an activist overlapped completely. In her memoir *Just as I Thought,* Paley recalls a friend asking her why she never wrote anything about menopause. *Hmm,* thought Paley, who was then sixty-eight. As a peace activist and women's-rights activist, she could barely remember menopause, because for her it occurred when she was so knee-deep in fighting for those causes that it hardly registered.

"Writing for me has always come from being bugged—agitated by a life, a speaking voice, an idea. I've asked some of my age mates, old friends, and they feel pretty much the same way," she writes. "We were busy. Life was heightened by opposition, and hope was essential."

Reading Paley and others like her can raise your consciousness and heighten your sense of possibility, as well. Even if these writers don't send you to the barricades, they can turn you into a more informed and responsible citizen. If you take Molly Ivins's advice, you'll also have more fun.

"Lord, let your laughter ring forth. Be outrageous, ridicule the fraidy-cats, rejoice in all the oddities that freedom can produce," she wrote in a 1993 *Mother Jones* essay entitled "The Fun's in the Fight." "And when you get through kickin' ass and celebratin' the sheer joy of a good fight, be sure to tell those who come after how much fun it was."

FOR THE TWENTY-FIRST CENTURY

1. *The Extreme Future: The Top Trends That Will Reshape the World for the Next 20 Years* by James Canton. In the next two decades global futurist Canton envisions a postoil economy, a multicultural and predominantly female workforce, a stronger China, teleporting, nanotechnology, and climate change. Even if he's wrong, says Canton, "future readiness" is key: "When there is no Future Vision, there is nothing to work toward creating." Or, quoting Yogi Berra: "You've got to be very careful if you don't know where you're going, because you might not get there."

2. *A Disorder Peculiar to the Country: A Novel* by Ken Kalfus. Irony is the hardest thing to teach, but if you have the knack for it, you'll love this post-9/11 novel. For New Yorkers Joyce and Marshall Harriman, even though he worked in the Twin Towers, its collapse merely mirrors the apocalypse that has consumed

LOOKING TO THE TWENTY-SECOND AND BEYOND

Ursula K. Le Guin writes speculative fiction, and don't call it sci-fi. Le Guin rejects that label, which too often evokes images of robots and nerdy young guys—and some very bad writing. As an award-winning writer, she has spent nearly a half-century elevating a genre that doesn't always get much respect.

More important than labels, though, is why Le Guin chooses that form. Having interviewed the author and written about her work as a journalist, I enrolled in her summer writing seminar several years ago to better understand the imaginative writing she advocates. These close-ups revealed how deeply Le Guin's "thought experiments" are rooted in her progressive political convictions. With futuristic flights of fancy, she imagines the world as it could or should be—a place where sexism and racism don't exist.

For example, in her 1969 novel, *The Left Hand of Darkness*, characters switch from male to female and back with the same ease as real people change clothes. It was Le Guin's way of exploring what the world would be like if gender didn't matter. In her memorable short story "Sur: A Summary Report of the Yelcho Expedition to the Antarctic, 1909–10," she tweaked the patriarchy by imagining an all-woman trek to the South Pole that takes place shortly after the great rush of male explorers. The successful trip had to be kept hush-hush for the sake of the oversized egos of the men who came before.

In her long writing career, Le Guin has covered a wide swath, including poetry and fiction for young people. But her feminist convictions have been a constant. The latest evidence: *Lavinia*, a novel that sees the world of Virgil's epic poem *The Aeneid* through the title character's eyes. Even going backward in time, the writer finds a way to make her case that women's voices should be heard.

~ Ellen

their marriage. Getting even and getting the kids—not to mention a great settlement—is the name of their game. Through this prism of discord, Kalfus deftly charts a newly anxious world where the enemy may include not only persons unknown, but also your spouse.

3. *Wikinomics: How Mass Collaboration Changes Everything* by Don Tapscott and Anthony D. Williams. Moving beyond "crowd wisdom," the global cooperation made possible by the Internet is creating profound structural changes in the workplace. New enterprises like Wikipedia, the collectively edited online encyclopedia, as well as traditional companies like Boeing are learning to profit from such "weapons of mass collaboration" as "openness, peering, sharing, and acting globally." Even this book, a "call to arms to create a wikinomics community," is an ongoing collaborative undertaking (see www.wikinomics.com).

4. *The Unbinding* by Walter Kirn. This novel shows you the Orwellian side of cyber culture. Kent Selkirk mans the phone for a subscriber service that's the ultimate human tracking system, monitoring customers' whereabouts and vital signs. The company's network also comes in handy for hitting on his neighbor, Sabrina. Although Kent claims to be more than the sum of "the calls he makes, the letters he writes or the e-mails he sends out," his soul seems to have stripped a few gears while he's playing Big Brother. Alas, Big Brother is also watching him. So long, privacy.

5. *The Red Queen: Sex and the Evolution of Human Nature* by Matt Ridley. "Just say no" becomes "just ask why" for evolutionary biologists, and their current theory for sex posits gene mixing. This occurs when female and male merge to produce offspring, which keeps humans one step ahead of parasites and infection. It also assigns specific roles in the breeding game, underlining that women are hardwired differently. We're cool with that, as long as how we act as sexual beings isn't applied to every job.

6. *Amusing Ourselves to Death* by Neil Postman. Twenty years after it was first printed, this book returns to pose the same relevant questions: What happens when we become infatuated with new technologies, especially TV and the Internet? What do we gain and lose? Postman takes on the "dangerous nonsense" that passes for serious content in the media and warns of a "Brave New World," à la Huxley, where "truth is drowned in a sea of irrelevance." Spin doctors, be gone! Hurray for a print-based culture and a marketplace that favors the rationality of ideas over the seduction of images.

7. *Blood Matters: From Inherited Illness to Designer Babies, How the World and I Found Ourselves in the Future of the Gene* by Masha Gessen. Gessen's interest in genes isn't just academic. A genetic test proved that she, like many Ashkenazi Jews, carries the mutation gene for breast and ovarian cancer that killed her mother. The ethics of spare baby parts and stem cell research may still be hotly debated, but screening embryos is already common practice in Israel, says Gessen: "There is no stopping the genetic future you say is so scary, because that future is already here."

8. *Brown: The Last Discovery of America* by Richard Rodriguez. "I write about race in America in hopes of undermining the notion of race in America," begins Rodriguez in this rumination on an increasingly blended society. Most Americans associate brown with Latin America, but he sees it as a color that can complete the country's "founding palette" of red, black, and white, "the meeting of the Indian, the African and the European." The combination of the conquistador and the Indian, brown is "a reminder of conflict. And of reconciliation."

9. *The Great Awakening: Reviving Faith and Politics in a Post-Religious Right America* by Jim Wallis. Drawing on the history of social movements inspired by faith, preacher and activist Wallis says America is on the verge of another such groundswell. His "common-good agenda" addresses poverty, the environment, and the "multiple assaults on human life and dignity" (a catch-all for such hot-button issues as abortion and gay rights). Social transformation, Wallis notes, springs from personal transformation. Spiritual renewal, Christian or other, is where it all starts.

10. *The World Without Us* by Alan Weisman. Science writer Weisman doesn't want humankind to perish. Instead, he wants his two-legged pals to get more sensitive to nature by imagining Spaceship Earth minus our tinkering, the results of which would disappear incredibly fast if we went poof. Meticulous research backs up a picture of how signs of progress vanish into a landscape of deep, dark forests and alluvial plains, leaving PCBs as our footprint. Moral of the story: Don't fool with Mother Nature. One sneeze, and she'll knock your version of progress off the map.

THAT SAY, "GET INVOLVED"

1. *Pay It Forward* by Catherine Ryan Hyde. As usual, the book is better than the movie, so head straight to the print version. This novel revolves around a twelve-year-old hero named Trevor McKinney, whose extra-credit social-studies project reverberates across the nation. The idea is that when you help someone else, the generosity is repaid with kindnesses to three others. And even though his teacher, Reuben, cautions, "You can't orchestrate, love, Trevor," the boy does just that by linking mentor and mom in a romance that transcends the tough luck of their past lives.

2. *The Zookeeper's Wife: A War Story* by Diane Ackerman. "Somewhere between doing and not doing, everyone's conscience finds its own level," Ackerman observes in her story about Jan and Antonina Zabinski, Christian keepers of the Warsaw Zoo when the Nazis invaded Poland in 1939. As the country became a Nazi killing field (for people and animals alike), the couple risked death to harbor Jews escaping the Warsaw Ghetto. With deprivation and death at hand, Antonina turned into a cunning housewife, feeding three hundred "guests" before war's end.

3. *Adventure Divas: Searching the Globe for a New Kind of Heroine* by Holly Morris. This book is only one part of an enterprise (google "adventure divas") based on finding risk-taking women in the far corners of the Earth. Morris's own example—even when hanging on for dear life in a camel race, or wishing she'd brought a tampon in the Borneo jungle—proves the value of having a dream and working hard for it. She spotlights a woman fighting the sex trade in India and an Islamic feminist in Iran. She returns home with a broader cultural perspective and convinced that divas are on the rise.

4. *Indecision* by Benjamin Kunkel. Good political fiction is rare, but rarer still is a novel like this one that manages to make the case for social justice and make you laugh. Dwight Wilmerding, twenty-eight, suffers from abulia (an inability to make decisions). Traveling to Ecuador, he finds not one but two antidotes: love and a sense of purpose. "The weird thing about freedom to choose," Wilmerding warns his well-heeled classmates in a speech at his college reunion, "would seem to be that no one knows what to do with it unless they give it to others."

5. *Three Cups of Tea: One Man's Mission to Promote Peace . . . One School at a Time* by Greg Mortenson and David Oliver Relin. In this rendering, Greg Mortenson deserves sainthood more than Mother Teresa: The former mountain climber helped save one of his own, cherished his epileptic sister, then trumped all previous good deeds with a school-building project in northern Pakistan. But he seems to be the real deal: When Mortenson stretches out on a prayer rug to show respect for his Muslim hosts, you get the picture of a guy who works at ground level to push books, not bullets, in the war against terrorism.

6. *Creating a World Without Poverty: How Social Business Can Transform Our Lives* by Muhammad Yunus. Nobel Peace Prize winner Yunus has lifted millions out of poverty through Grameen Bank's collateral-free loans. Now the "banker to the poor" hopes to put "poverty in a museum" with his next Big Idea: social businesses, companies that place social good before profit. Is capitalism with a human face a pipe dream? A joint venture between France's Groupe Danone and the bank already exists, producing low-cost yogurt for Bangladesh's poor. "We can refigure our world if we can reconfigure our mindset."

7. *The Last Flight of the Scarlet Macaw: One Woman's Fight to Save the World's Most Beautiful Bird* by Bruce Barcott. You've got to marvel at Sharon Matola, who'll hold a tarantula and used to wrestle big cats for a living. But how's this for bravery: As the zookeeper of Belize, she led the charge to save nesting habitat by fighting a proposed dam in that Central American country. "Every once in a while," Barcott writes, "I meet a rare subspecies of human who offers hope. It's almost never a politician or a scientist. It's almost always a woman without credentials."

8. *The Devil Came on Horseback: Bearing Witness to the Genocide in Darfur* by Brian Steidle and Gretchen Steidle Wallace. Seeking adventure, ex–U.S. Marine Steidle took a job with an international force to monitor a ceasefire in Sudan. But instead of preventing conflict, he watched helplessly as government-armed nomads—"janjaweed" ("the devil on a horse")—massacred innocent civilians. In an account based on field reports, e-mails to his sister Gretchen, and photographs, he describes his evolving

LEND A BOOK, CHANGE THE WORLD

Readers often believe they can make the world a better place by lending certain books. I know I do.

In high school, I wanted everyone to read John Steinbeck's *East of Eden,* a novel that told me that I was the architect of my own destiny. In college, I was wowed by *The Autobiography of Malcolm X: As Told to Alex Haley* by Malcolm X. It introduced me to a world far removed from my own, and I wanted others to have the same eye-opening experience.

I've given away novels including Milan Kundera's *The Unbearable Lightness of Being,* Manuel Puig's *Kiss of the Spider Woman,* and Primo Levi's *The Monkey Wrench,* hoping friends would love them as much as I did.

"Each man has a bit of the evangelist in him," longtime *New York Times* book critic Anatole Broyard wrote in his essay "Lending Books," "and when a book moves me I want to put it into everyone's pocket."

Of course, it's called "lending," but when a book is given away, it probably won't be seen again. In *Zuckerman Unbound* (by Philip Roth), Zuckerman's brother marries a girl as the only way to repossess a book he lent her.

These days you can lend your books over the Internet at book swapping sites that engage in *bookcrossing,* a term that was added to the *Concise Oxford English Dictionary* in 2004:

Bookcrossing: *n. the practice of leaving a book in a public place to be picked up and read by others, who then do likewise.*

The practice was inspired by BookCrossing.com, a free online book club. On the site are the three Rs of BookCrossing: read, register, and release. Book lovers read a good book, register it on the site, and then release it either by giving it to a friend or leaving it in a public place like a park bench or coffee shop. The movement of the book can be tracked on the site—or you can check the site to track down a book. Paradoxically, claims BookCrossing, the number who *buy* books based on seeing the book reviews on the site as the books change hands is greater than those who *find* the books.

There are always those naysayers, like Anatole France, who warn against book lending: "Never lend books—nobody ever returns them; the only books I have in my library are those which people have lent me."

~ **Margo**

sense of outrage: "When the genocide in Darfur has ended, what will you say you did to stop it?"

9. *An Atomic Romance* by Bobbie Ann Mason. The romance of this novel's title is between Reed Futrell, a hunky engineer, and Julie Jensen, a brainy biologist, who meet in an elevator, bantering about the theory of space-time. Their on-again, off-again relationship hits a serious snag when Reed ignores Julie's warnings about a radiation leak at the Kentucky plant where he works and his father was killed years before. After Julie disappears and his mom has a stroke, Reed rethinks what's important to him. "The universe tantalized him and affronted him, ripping him out of his own corner."

10. *Hope in the Dark: Untold Histories, Wild Possibilities* by Rebecca Solnit. Cultural historian Solnit urges fellow activists to work for a better world no matter how dark the future appears. Pointing to the positive changes that have occurred in the past five decades, from the fall of the Berlin Wall to the rise of a worldwide antiwar movement, she warns against giving up too easily. No one can know the full consequences of even the smallest acts, she says. "It's always too soon to go home. And it's always too soon to calculate effect."

TO SAVE THE PLANET

1. *The Creation: An Appeal to Save Life on Earth* by E. O. Wilson. Noted entomologist and ant expert Wilson was raised as an evangelical Christian but now puts his faith in science. In this slim book, writing a letter to a fictional "Southern Baptist Pastor," he proposes that religious people and nonbelievers put aside their differences and work together to help save the planet. "The defense of the living Nature is a universal value. It doesn't rise from nor does it promote any religious or ideological dogma. Rather, it serves without discrimination the interests of all humanity."

2. *Return to Wild America: A Yearlong Search for the Continent's Natural Soul* by Scott Weidensaul. Commemorating a 30,000-mile, midcentury trek by world-renowned birder Roger Tory Peterson and British naturalist James Fisher, Weidensaul covers the same terrain to trace the progress. Although not happy with all he sees, he skips the Cassandra role to report that more parks and refuges have been created, some threatened species have seen a comeback, and the environmental movement has built a full head of steam (using alternate fuels, of course).

3. *Firekeeper: Selected Poems* by Pattiann Rogers. A poet's sensuality combines with the powers of a scientist's observation to make Rogers's verse notable for its depictions of the natural world. The new edition of *Firekeeper,* first published in 1994, literally sees red in "Suppose Your Father Was a Redbird." Here such disparate objects as birds, moths, and the setting sun are united in the same landscape, so that: "Your sudden visions you might interpret as the uncreasing / Of heaven, the bones of the sky spread, / The conceptualized wing of the mind untangling."

4. *Farewell, My Subaru: An Adventure in Local Living* by Doug Fine. Yes, environmentalists have a sense of humor. At least, Fine does, which helped immensely when he shoved his lifestyle in reverse to prove that "a regular American can still live like a regular American, only on far fewer fossil fuels." At age thirty-six, newly ensconced on his Funky Butte Ranch in New Mexico, he relies on solar power, goats Natalie and Melissa, and a truck powered by vegetable oil. What's amazing is that shrinking his carbon footprint didn't put a dent in his active social life: Going green gets the girls.

5. *The Future of Ice: A Journey Into Cold* by Gretel Ehrlich. What if global warming caused winter to disappear? Ehrlich pondered that question while living six months in remote lands

SHOTS HEARD ROUND THE WORLD

Those of us who love books know that books make a difference in our own lives. But can they really change the world? Two green classics did, with a winning combination: an environmental cause, a passionate woman writer, and a lyrical title.

In 1945, shortly after the publication of Marjory Stoneman Douglas's *The Everglades: A River of Grass*, 2 million acres were set aside to form the Everglades National Park, the first national park preserved primarily for its abundance and variety of life, rather than for scenic or historic value.

I first heard about Douglas when I moved to St. Petersburg, Florida, in 1990. At age one hundred, she was a local hero. Her autobiography, *Voice of the River*, had been published just three years before. In the foreword, her cowriter, John Rothschild, describes an eighty-eight-year-old Douglas lobbying for "her" Everglades in huge dark glasses and a floppy hat that "made her look like Scarlet O'Hara as played by Igor Stravinsky." She lived to be 108.

Rachel Carson's *Silent Spring*, published in 1962, prompted a presidential inquiry into the safety of pesticides. I read *Silent Spring* when I was in high school, as impressed by it as John F. Kennedy had been. Carson, a marine biologist who had written three books about the sea, including a best seller, *The Sea Around Us*, was much less flamboyant than Douglas. While working on *Silent Spring*, she discovered she had breast cancer. She quietly underwent a radical mastectomy and radiation treatment. Within two years of the book's publication, she was dead.

These two green queens may have had different styles, but both understood the importance of stirring prose. "There are no other Ever-

glades in the world," Douglas writes in the opening lines of her sentimental ode to America's wetlands. "They are, they have always been,
one of the unique regions of the earth; remote, never wholly known."

The opening of Carson's *Silent Spring*, labeled "A Fable for Tomorrow," also was crafted for maximum dramatic effect. First painting
the picture of a "town in the heart of America where all life seemed
to live in harmony with its surroundings," Carson then writes of something going terribly wrong:

"A strange blight crept over the area and everything began to
change. . . . There was a strange stillness. The birds, for example—
where had they gone. Many people spoke of them, puzzled and dis-
turbed. The feeding stations in the backyards were deserted. A few
birds seen anywhere were moribund; they trembled violently and
could not fly. It was a spring without voices."

~ Margo

of deep cold, including the earth's polar ends. Here, she offers
vivid descriptions of roughing it on ice combined with startling
facts about the ecological importance of the cold season. Her ru-
minations, she admits, are "both ode and lament, a wild-time
song and elegy, and a cry for help—not for me, but for the tern,
the ice cap, the polar bear, and the lenga forest."

6. *An Inconvenient Truth: The Planetary Emergency of Global
Warming and What We Can Do About It* by Al Gore. The Chinese
expression for crisis consists of two characters, the symbols for
danger and opportunity, Gore reminds us in this environmental
jeremiad. A companion to the movie that won the former vice

president the Nobel Peace Prize, this volume, with its facts, charts, and shocking photos, offers ample evidence of the dangers of global warming. (Check out Florida under water.) The time to stop it is now. "Inconvenient truths do not go away just because they are not seen."

7. *The Monkey Wrench Gang* by Edward Abbey. Published in 1975 and dedicated to Ned Ludd of Luddite fame, Abbey's raucous novel about a motley group of eco-raiders can be read as a wake-up call on behalf of nature or a dangerous incitement to violence ("Violence," says one gang member, "it's as American as apple pie"). Historian Douglas Brinkley, introducing the book's twenty-fifth anniversary edition, compares it to Rachel Carson's *Silent Spring* and Thomas Paine's *Common Sense,* works written "to jar the soul." Remember, says Brinkley, Abbey's loveable pranksters "kill only machines, not people."

8. *The Wild Trees: A Story of Passion and Daring* by Richard Preston. Afraid of heights? If so, you'll be all the more amazed by the arborists and nature buffs who scale the tallest redwoods and Douglas firs. Preston learned the ropes to help explain the derring-do and scientific contributions of his fellow skywalkers, whose bird's-eye view helps them map the western forests. One climber exemplified their dedication: After falling a hundred feet (nearly twice the height at which you're expected to survive), he returned to climb the same tree a few months later.

9. *Evidence of Things Unseen* by Marianne Wiggins. This novel is a cautionary tale wrapped around the atom's power and the dan-

gers of science. It's also a love story that travels from first blush to a bond forged in grief. Fos, the main character, covers the distance from lighting trenches in one war to advancing development of the bomb in the next. His work with radiation exposes his beloved Opal to unacceptable doses in the decades before Japanese cities were consumed with flashes of light. "Of all the things that we could do with the natural wonder we call science," he marvels. "Make a goddam killing weapon."

10. *The Myth of Solid Ground: Earthquakes, Prediction, and the Fault Line Between Reason and Faith* by David Ulin. Earthquakes are not about us, California journalist Ulin concludes in this quirky, insightful look at the unsettling phenomenon of shifting ground. They belong to cosmic, not human, time. The theories of seismologists and earthquake "predictors" are as shaky as the Earth: "To live with earthquakes is to have one foot in the present and the other in the deepest reaches of the past. It is to find a balance, to understand that everything is always up for grabs."

THAT SEE THROUGH A SCIENTIST'S EYES

1. *Passionate Minds: Emilie du Chatelet, Voltaire and the Great Love Affair of the Enlightenment* by David Bodanis. At a time when other women of her stripe chose between the intellectual sterility of convent or court, du Chatelet taught herself analytic geometry and advanced Newtonian physics. No wonder Voltaire fell in love

with her: Their partnership was a true meeting of minds, with hers arguably superior. Set against the corruption and infidelity that marked eighteenth-century France, this story is the perfect response to anyone who thinks women can't do math and science.

2. *Longitude: The True Story of a Lone Genius Who Solved the Greatest Scientific Problem of his Time* by Dava Sobel. Science made simple: If anyone pioneered the concept with style, it was Sobel, whose obscurity-to-riches story launched a publishing trend with this small book. It describes how sea explorers used "dead reckoning" to gauge location until the English Parliament offered cash for a better way. After John Harrison spent years developing his chronometer, King George III took on his cause, marine time-keeping became the rage, and Great Britain ruled the waves.

3. *The Map That Changed the World: William Smith and the Birth of Modern Geology* by Simon Winchester. Like Harrison, fellow Brit Smith didn't get full credit for his achievements until life's end. But en route this blacksmith's son and canal builder rose to gentleman status while deducing that the strata of rock and sediment on his stony isle were key to the Earth's formation. Class consciousness, a nation's need for coal, and the fad of using fossils as drawing-room art fold neatly into this window on one of the bright minds of the Industrial Revolution.

4. *The Strange Case of the Broad Street Pump: John Snow and the Mystery of Cholera* by Sandra Hempel. Writing nonfiction like a novelist, Hempel vividly re-creates a neighborhood in Victorian England that's wracked with cholera. There, Dr. John Snow disproved the then-accepted wisdom that the disease was airborne by doggedly linking the afflicted to a public water source. Dirty water was the disease's real conduit. His methods changed forever the way infectious diseases are tracked. See what you get when you think outside the box (or, in this case, inside the Broad Street Pump)?

5. *The Book About Blanche and Marie* by Per Olov Enquist. Real people and real tragedies lurk behind those Nobel prizes, as this dreamlike novel demonstrates. Inspired by notebooks found among the papers of Blanche Wittman, Marie Curie's lab assistant, Enquist offers a reconstruction of their confidences. Both were burned by the hot flame of passion in love scandals that ended badly. Both were poisoned by the "blue light" of radiation (Wittman lost three limbs before she died; Curie succumbed to radiation exposure). Enquist: "What is the chemical formula for desire?"

6. *Einstein: A Biography* by Jürgen Neffe. Here's an idea: In addition to reading Walter Isaacson's bestselling version of the life of the man who changed the way we see the universe, try its Prussian parallel, which is more warts-and-all and mindful of Einstein's roots. Teaching assistants at Princeton had to know German because Einstein spoke so little English. Neffe likens him to Oskar in Gunther Grass's novel *The Tin Drum,* who never grows up—similarly, he claims, Einstein retained a sense of childish wonder that made him open to discovery.

7. *Polio: An American Story* by David M. Oshinsky. In this readable account, Pulitzer Prize winner Oshinsky focuses on the rivalry between two giant egos—Jonas Salk and Alfred Sabin—in the race to eradicate polio. Salk introduced the killed-virus vaccine in 1955; Sabin, the live-virus alternative a few years later. Oshinsky re-creates the climate of those literally feverish years of outlandish "cures," the March of Dimes poster child, and efforts by FDR, a polio victim himself, to raise public awareness. "No disease drew as much attention, or struck the same terror, as polio."

8. *Living Time: Faith and Facts to Transform Your Cancer Journey* by Bernadine Healy. Behind the self-help title, you'll find a doctor who ran both the National Institutes of Health and the Red Cross. In 1999, after she was diagnosed with a brain tumor, she used her medical training to fight for her life. During surgery, she read aloud to ensure no scalpel would invade the speech center of her brain. In follow-up, she trusted both her head and her heart. This book combines her story with a primer on cancer and an upbeat progress report. "Don't let grim words and numbers rule your life."

9. *Train Your Mind, Change Your Brain: How a New Science Reveals Our Extraordinary Potential to Transform Ourselves* by Sharon Begley. Adult brains, once thought to be static, can change themselves, says *Wall Street Journal* science writer Begley in this readable book about monks and the cutting-edge science of neuroplasticity: "Like sand on the beach, the brain bears the footprints of the decisions we have made, the skills we have learned, the actions we have taken." Even thoughts, says Begley, can alter your brain structure—an idea Buddhist meditators have been exploring for millennia.

10. *Voyage of the Narwhal* by Andrea Barrett. In this epic novel, Barrett examines the not-so-noble forces that drove the all-male "scientific" explorations so popular in the mid-nineteenth century: Ambition. Machismo. Racism. The attitude of the crew of the *Narwhal,* a sailing ship exploring the Arctic, toward the indigenous Inuits they encounter in the frozen north is shocking, as are the racial theories of this pre–Civil War period. But when naturalist Erasmus Wells discusses Charles Darwin's emerging theories of evolution and natural selection, you see glimpses of the scientific ferment to come.

THAT MAKE WAR (AND PEACE)

1. *Peace* by Richard Bausch. This novella is set in the brutal winter of 1944 near the Abbey of Mount Cassino, site of an Allied bombing that killed hundreds of Italian noncombatants during World War II. In Bausch's story, only one civilian, a prostitute, is killed, shot in the head by an American sergeant after two of his men died in a crossfire with her German companion. Her execution echoes the dilemma raised by events at Mount Cassino: Can there really be morality in wartime? Bausch explores this vexing question with a spareness that will haunt you.

2. *The Warrior: A Mother's Story of a Son at War* by Frances Richey. Here's a case in point: Freud said that the most perfect relationship exists between a mother and son, and poet Richey eloquently expresses this idea as she contemplates her boy, a West Point grad, and his departure for Iraq. Love and worry braid together, like two sides of the same coin, as she remembers moments from the past and imagines the hardships and danger of battle. "Isn't that your job? / To whisper in the ear of / any god who'll listen: *Please, / protect him.*"

3. *The Homecoming* by Bernhard Schlink. War turns honest people into liars, and liars into opportunists. That's the trajectory laid out by German writer Schlink, who's known for examining the Nazi legacy through fiction, most notably in his Oprah-blessed best seller *The Reader.* Here Schlink features a fatherless young man whose own father was lost in the war and is obsessed with stories about others like him. Turning over the stones of the past, he discovers a law professor in America who becomes a stand-in for the former Nazis who after the war erased their connections to the Third Reich.

4. *When the Emperor Was Divine* by Julie Otsuka. "The Christmas tree was up, and the whole house smelled of pine, and from his window the boy had watched as they led his father out across the lawn in his bathrobe and slippers." In the months after Pearl Harbor, 120,000 Japanese-Americans were relocated, and this spare novel records the experience through the eyes of one family. Re-creating the environment of fear and the victimization that followed, Otsuka offers a fitting heir to Joy Kogowa's *Obasan* and a cautionary tale for our own time.

5. *In the Shadow of No Towers* by Art Spiegelman. Spiegelman, who won a Pulitzer Prize for his haunting Maus books on the Holocaust, again turns to making comix (the *x* signaling that these picture stories are not for kids), this time to sort out his feeling about 9/11 and its "hijacked" aftermath. "Synopsis: In our last episode, as you might remember, the world ended . . . ," he writes, mimicking old comic strips. Interspersing characters from those strips with his own drawings, he re-creates that day, beginning with "the image of the looming north tower's glowing bones just before it vaporized."

6. *Baghdad Burning: Girl Blog From Iraq* **Volumes I and II** by Riverbend. The U.S. invasion of Iraq has prompted a battalion of books, but if you really want to know what it feels like to live through war, read the blogs of Riverbend, the online name of an Iraqi woman from a mixed Sunni and Shiite family. She describes a world of ducking sniper fire and religious fanatics, of blackouts and boredom, in postings between September 2003 and October 2007, when her family fled to Syria. "We have 9/11s on a daily basis."

7. *Soldier's Heart: Reading Literature Through Peace and War at West Point* by Elizabeth D. Samet. Samet, a civilian who teaches English to West Point cadets, works at one of the few campuses touched deeply by the war in Iraq. There, she has developed an acute sense of how the nature of war and sacrifice collides with the individual value of her soldier scholars. "The allure of military life and its heroic promise seem indestructible, but nothing threatens the romance of *war* more effectively than war itself."

8. *The Lemon Tree: An Arab, a Jew, and the Heart of the Middle East* by Sandy Tolan. Home is where the heart is, Tolan decided, so he used the idea to frame the Arab-Israeli conflict, telling the history of a house in a small Israeli town. Built in 1936 by Palestinian Ahmad Khairi (he planted the lemon tree), it became the home of Jewish immigrants after he and his family were uprooted in the 1948 war. Tolan is respectful to the claims of Ahmad's son, Bashir, and the olive branch extended by present occupant Dalia Eshkenazi Landau. Sadly, his story only highlights how intractable their two positions are.

9. *Nonviolence Explained to My Children* by Jacques Semelin. "Nonviolence is not passivity," Parisian political science professor Semelin says in this slim volume, part of a French series on explaining difficult subjects to kids. "It's a way of being and behaving in conflict situations that respects the other person." Nonviolence, he admits, can't work miracles. But in a question-and-answer session with his two teenage daughters, he describes how to "fight without violence," citing historic nonviolent actions, from Montgomery to Gdansk, that brought about change: "You could call it 'the power of the weak.'"

10. *A Human Being Died That Night: A South African Story of Forgiveness* by Pumla Gobodo-Madikizela. On behalf of South Africa's Truth and Reconciliation Commission, founded to heal the wounds of apartheid, clinical psychologist Gobodo-Madikizela interviews Eugene de Kock, one of the former regime's most notorious torturers, now in a maximum-security prison. Expecting to confront the face of evil, she finds instead someone "capable of feeling, crying, and knowing pain." In this honest and moving account of how the TRC worked to achieve reconciliation, she contemplates what an immensely complicated task it is to forgive the unforgivable.

THAT HEAR US ROAR

1. *Becoming Judy Chicago: A Biography of the Artist* by Gail Levin. When Judy Gerowitz (later known as Judy Chicago) founded the Feminist's Art Project at Fresno State College in the '70s, women artists didn't often make it into art history textbooks. Now, none would be complete without mentioning *The Dinner Party,* her 1979 installation of erotic place settings celebrating thirty-nine women in history. In this massive biography, Levin traces the life of this controversial pioneer of an art based on women's life experiences. What is feminist art? As Chicago once told a reporter: "You know a woman did it."

2. *The Lives of the Muses: Nine Women and the Artists They Inspired* by Francine Prose. Borrowing from Greek mythology, Prose pinpoints nine "goddesses" who inspired famous men. "Serial muse" Lou Andreas-Salome gets extra points for her relationships (platonic and not) with three geniuses: philosopher Nietszche, poet Rilke, psychiatrist Freud. Yoko Ono gets sarcastic treatment as the survivor who rewrote history, giving John Lennon the supporting role. Gala Dali, wife of Salvador, had him spellbound: "It is mostly with your blood, Gala, that I paint my pictures," he said.

3. *Falling Angels* by Tracy Chevalier. The birth of women's suffrage in Great Britain is turned into a period-piece novel that uses a chorus of female voices to capture the flavor of Edwardian England. Untold secrets lurk upstairs and downstairs as the cemetery becomes a center of social and sexual engagement (with thanks to Queen Victoria for "elevating mourning to such ridiculous heights"). Kitty Coleman is the unhappy housewife who feels trapped in a golden cage until she discovers the movement, leaving her husband and daughter to fend for themselves. Kitty's resolve leads to a fate that fits the times perfectly.

4. *America's Women: 400 Years of Dolls, Drudges, Helpmates and Heroines* by Gail Collins. The first woman to head *The New York Times* editorial board, Collins has an unorthodox way of looking at the past, as "Scorpion Tongues," her playful survey of the history of gossip, demonstrated. She likes to ask basic questions. And we mean basic. How did colonial women deal with menstruation and BO? How did Eleanor Dare's husband convince her in 1587 to come to America, where no European woman had ever been? Collins digs until she finds an answer: "Eleanor Dare was either extraordinarily adventurous or easily led."

5. *Breaking Clean* by Judy Blunt. "If 'ranch wife' was a job, I'd spent my entire life in training," Blunt writes in this memoir about growing up, getting married, and giving birth in the tough, male-dominated landscape of eastern Montana. A decade into the marriage, the bond wore thin, tested by the needs and dreams she tried to express to a husband who wanted to reclaim the woman he thought he married. With a new divorce and three scared kids, she left for a new life on the other side of the mountains—"not easier, but different," she writes. "And it's enough."

6. *A Life Less Ordinary* by Baby Halder. This memoir, translated from Hindi, finds triumph in adversity few Americans could imagine. The first inkling the author has that she's about to be married comes when her stepmother starts smearing her with tumeric paste. She is twelve years old. Fast-forward past three babies and years of servitude to her husband, and you find Baby so determined to educate her children that she goes to work as a domestic. Through luck, her employer is an educated man who detects her yearning to learn and gives her the tools to write her story.

7. *Well-Behaved Women Seldom Make History* by Laurel Thatcher Ulrich. Harvard history prof Ulrich actually coined the phrase that she uses as the title of this book. Well-behaved or not, the subjects she profiles are women who left a record, from writers such as Christine de Pizan and Virginia Woolf to feminists early and late, to the collective voices and artists known to history as Anon. But forget the idea of a universal sisterhood, she says. "If history is to enlarge our understanding of human experience, it must include stories that dismay as well as inspire."

8. *From Eve to Dawn: A History of Women in the World, Volume I: Origins: From Prehistory to the First Millennium* by Marilyn French. How did men end up with all the power, especially power over women? French asks in this first of four volumes of her massive but highly readable history of women. Her answer: "Patriarchy was the result of a revolution, the world's first." You may not agree that men should take all the blame, but as novelist Margaret Atwood says in her introduction, the "appalling extremes of human behavior and male weirdness" French presents as evidence can't be dismissed.

9. *The Ordeal of Elizabeth Marsh: A Woman in World History* by Linda Colley. Here Princeton history prof Colley tracks Marsh, an eighteenth-century Englishwoman, making the case that large historical waves often converge with the ripples of individual lives. To wit: Marsh and her wandering ways personified her nation's seaborne slant and newfound outlets for entrepreneurial pluck, such as the travel writing she took up. Yes, her story shows how male fortunes framed a woman's life. Yet, Colley emphasizes, Marsh worked the system better than most.

10. *Women's Letters: America from the Revolutionary War to the Present* edited by Lisa Grunwald and Stephen J. Adler. Rachel Revere sends support to her husband after his famous ride. Joan Baez tells the IRS: "I do not believe in war." Martha Stewart asks her sentencing judge to "consider all the good I have done." Women's letters rarely just exchange information, say the editors. "Instead, they tell stories; they tell secrets; they shout and scold, bitch and soothe, whisper and worry, console and advise, gossip and argue, compete and compare." Here's your chance to read someone else's mail.

THAT POKE THE POWERFUL

1. The Daily Show with Jon Stewart Presents *America (The Book): A Citizen's Guide to Democracy Inaction* by Jon Stewart and the writers of *The Daily Show*. In this hilarious spoof of civics textbooks, Stewart & Co. explain how Congress ("the gastrointestinal tract of the body politic") and elections ("Learn why your vote counts, but not nearly as much as your money") really work. Successfully walking a tightrope between frat-boy high jinks and biting political satire, they disrobe power—figuratively and literally (check out the photograph of all nine Supreme Court judges naked).

2. *The Nine: Inside the Secret World of the Supreme Court* by Jeffrey Toobin. Speaking of the high court, *New Yorker* writer and legal analyst Toobin puts his analytical tools to the test to scrutinize the most powerful unelected body in the land (even more than D.C. lobbyists!). This behind-the-scenes look parses cases (abortion and so forth), individual eccentricities (David Souter eats an apple a day, core and all), and the tilt of the court (five of the nine are practicing Catholics, and all trend conservative). Toobin's verdict: Public opinion has a moderating influence on ideology.

3. *Taking on the Trust: The Epic Battle of Ida Tarbell and John D. Rockefeller* by Steve Weinberg. The muckraker who invented investigative journalism is best known for breaking Rockefeller's hold on the American oil trade and turning him into a public villain. But this believer in the "great man" theory of history also put her stamp on Abraham Lincoln, solidifying his historical image as a frontiersman of uncompromising principles. Talk about the power of pen! Too bad Tarbell didn't buy the "great woman" theory: As others fought for universal suffrage, she sat on her hands.

4. *All Governments Lie!: The Life and Times of Rebel Journalist I. F. Stone* by Myra MacPherson. Here's another warts-and-all treatment of an extraordinary journalist, a man who said he looked like "a Jewish bullfrog" but was actually a bulldog in the world of Washington politics. Starting in the 1930s, Stone developed himself (and his newsletter) as a magnet for FBI surveillance and, in the era of TV, a public personality. Through the life of one grumpy guy with a printing press, McPherson illuminates both the sins of the left and its prescience about the risks of empire building.

5. *Skinny Dip* by Carl Hiaasen. The bad guys in a Carl Hiaasen mystery are never in doubt. The mystery is what horrific ways the *Miami Herald* journalist will dispatch his villains at novel's end. Here, the fictional scoundrels are Ron Hammernut, a large landowner who is polluting the Everglades with pesticide overruns, and Charles Perrone, a biologist covering up for him. Perrone also shoves his wife into the Atlantic on their anniversary cruise, but she swims into the arms of an ex-cop who helps her exact revenge. The villains' comeuppance? Let's just say it involves alligators.

6. *Florence of Arabia: A Novel* by Christopher Buckley. Justice is also swift in this comic novel, which turns public beheadings into the stuff of satire. Shocked by news that her friend was decapitated in Chop-Chop Square in Wasabia, a fictitious country ruled by fundamentalists, foreign service office Florence Farfaletti helps launch a TV show in the nearby emirate of Mutar (pronounced "mutter") to encourage women to revolt. The result? A fatwa against the station's staff and a death sentence for Farfaletti. Who said the revolution would be easy?

7. *Amazonia: Five Years at the Epicenter of the Dot.Com Juggernaut* by James Marcus. Here's a revolution of a different kind: the tech boom, as seen from the inside of the one-stop mega-shop Amazon.com. In 1996, book critic Marcus hired on, hoping to "preach the gospel of literature from the Internet pulpit." This naïve view quickly sank under assembly-line reviews and marketing blurbs as Amazon went public and Marcus made millions (alas, until the bust). Looking back at his five years atop the Internet bubble, he tracks a curious blend of art and commerce.

8. *The Natural History of the Rich: A Field Guide* by Richard Conniff. With his background as a naturalist, Conniff zooms in on a cultural subset, the wealthy, with impish glee and some (relatively) serious observations. One is that being rich draws gawkers and hangers-on, forcing the highly moneyed to hang together in self-defense and giving him such, well, rich material. Another is that the drive for dominance is hard-wired. And, finally, women seldom fare well at the top: It's hard to find equally well-heeled suitors, husbands tend to fool around, and family life is less about love than inheritance. Ah, the burdens!

9. *The Open Road: The Global Journey of the Fourteenth Dalai Lama* by Pico Iyer. A religious leader who tells people not to be distracted by religion, to push beyond doctrine "to something human," the globe-trotting, exiled head of Tibetan Buddhism tweaks the conscience of both haves and have-nots. In this profile by a self-described "skeptical journalist and nonbelonger," the Dalai Lama comes off as both holy and wholly practical. Like the Buddha, he sees himself only as a signpost. Or, as a Zen saying puts it, "just a finger pointing at a finger pointing at the moon."

10. *Gandhi: The Man, His People, and the Empire* by Rajmohan Gandhi. The author of this massive biography was twelve when his grandfather, Mahatma Gandhi, was assassinated in 1948. Now a professor at the University of Illinois, Rajmohan Gandhi offers a remarkably complete portrait, quirks and all, of the "bare, bony, bald, bespectacled" man whose nonviolent struggle drove the British out of India. Like Nelson Mandela, says the professor, Gandhi is a "man for all races." Shortly before his murder, he even forgave those who would do him harm: "I believe in loving my enemies."

VIII

BABES WITHOUT
BORDERS

After five years of marriage and a child, editor Anne Fadiman and her writer husband, George Howe Colt, finally decided to blend their libraries—a more profound intimacy than either of those other steps, she insists. A battle ensued over their different methods of cataloging books.

"George was a lumper. I am a splitter," explains Fadiman in *Ex Libris: Confessions of a Common Reader*, a collection of essays about her love of books. "His books commingled democratically, united under the all-inclusive flag of Literature. Some were vertical, some horizontal, and some actually placed *behind* others. Mine were balkanized by nationality and subject matter."

For Fadiman, some books just *belong* together. But, as her own example proves, categorizing has always been a tricky business.

The Book Babes' collaboration grows out of a desire to move away from the often arbitrary categories that limit readers: highbrow and lowbrow, popular and Literature with a capital

L. Nowhere was our challenge to defy labels greater than when it came to genre fiction, the romances and mysteries and historical recreations often branded as escapist literature. In the pages ahead, we deliver them with a twist.

Call us the genre busters. To liven up the worn-out labels used for those areas of popular reading—travel, mysteries, thrillers, and humor—we've come up with some strange and wonderful bedfellows.

To solve the crime, we rounded up the usual suspects and some you wouldn't suspect: P. D. James, the winner of mystery's Silver and Diamond Dagger awards, keeps good company with Kate Atkinson, who wins literary prizes like the Whitbread. In tracking down books that curdle our blood, we paired real-life thrills with imagined ones and mixed in such hybrids as Kathryn Harrison's *While They Slept: An Inquiry Into the Murder of a Family*, a combination memoir and true crime.

Most bookstores have a humor section filled with books that make you laugh. But what about a three-hankie section? Here are both books that make you laugh and ones that make you cry. Our travel section includes trips that take you along the Inland Passage and to Venice but also into the soul. We put you on the throne with biographies, historical fiction, the memoir of a queen, and a dishy chronicle of a princess.

We even include a list of books about books—our nod to that most hedonistic of activities, reading.

Genre busting is nothing new. Graham Greene originally called his suspense novels "entertainments." He wanted to separate them from his more weighty offerings, like *The Power and the Glory*, which he hoped would win him his literary bona fides. But as the distinction between his serious fiction and his "entertainments" became blurred, he (and his readers) abandoned the term. *The Quiet American* and *Our Man in Havana* feature many of the conventions of suspense, but they also contain elements associated with more highbrow works: Big Ideas, deeply developed characters, textured layers of meaning, and exquisite prose. Spy novels crossed the border into Literature.

J. R. R. Tolkien and C. S. Lewis, colleagues and friends at Oxford in the '30s and '40s, are famous for juggling scholarly writing and fiction that appealed to both children and adults. Neither believed that fiction had to taste like porridge to be great. Both elevated fantasy to new heights.

A philologist who was immersed in the origins of language, Tolkien was the picture of a stuffy don in his tweed coat smoking pipes, but he was comfortable talking about monsters and "faeries." For him, fantasy was not just a pastime for children but literature of the highest order. The "making or glimpsing of Otherworlds" is valuable, he argues in his essay "On Fairy-Stories," because it allows the reader to see his own situation from a different perspective. In his Lord of the Rings trilogy, the complex universe of Middle-earth is a world unto itself.

Lewis, who wrote his own defense of fairy tales ("Sometimes Fairy Stories May Say Best What's to Be Said"), took fantasy in another direction. An author of treatises on medieval literature and popular books on Christianity, Lewis incorporated his moral principles in his fantasy world—lying beyond a magic wardrobe in the *Chronicles of Narnia*. "You and I who still enjoy fairy tales have less reason to wish actual childhood back," the bespectacled Lewis wrote to a woman friend. "We have kept its pleasures and added some grown-up ones as well."

What's important in the debate about cataloging books is not how you set them on the shelf, but how you organize them in your mind. We avid readers, after all, are natural lumpers—if not on our bookshelves then on our bed stands, where Shakespeare and J. K. Rowling find equal footing. What class of people would you expect to be most preoccupied with and most hostile to, the idea of escapism? Lewis once asked Tolkien.

Lewis gave his own response: "Jailers."

THAT TAKE YOU AWAY

1. *The Bells in Their Silence: Travels Through Germany* by Michael Gorra. Gorra, a literary critic and English professor, equates travel writers to forensic scientists, "trying to piece together a culture out of a fragment or two of evidence." An extended stay in Germany lets him contemplate his own set of artifacts, if not riddles, regarding a nation of such interlocked extremes that it produced both Bach and the Holocaust. Travel offers the chance to examine your own habits and values, he says. "To journey out is to journey within."

2. *The Tenderness of Wolves* by Stef Penney. It is 1867. A French trapper has been scalped and his throat cut in Dover River, a small and until then peaceful Canadian outpost in territory dominated by the Hudson Bay Company. Tracks from the dead man's cabin point north toward the frozen tundra. A classic whodunit? Hardly. As a motley cast of characters plunge deeper into the isolated landscape to follow the murderer's trail, you'll find yourself caring less about the killer's identity and more about an even more lonely setting: the human heart.

3. *Passage to Juneau: A Sea and Its Meanings* by Jonathan Raban. Raban's solo journey up the Inland Passage from Seattle guides you through fickle tides and along fog-shrouded, forested shores. But, beyond the stunning vista, what makes this trip in his thirty-five-foot sailboat so memorable for the reader is the highly literate skipper at the helm. Raban smartly retraces Captain Vancouver's expedition (circa 1800), observes the devolution of coastal Indian culture, and quantifies the cost of his own absence from home. "Reading the Northwest nature writers," he notes, "I found myself an agnostic in their church." Raban's irreverence is a breath of fresh air.

4. *The Singular Pilgrim: Travels on Sacred Ground* by Rosemary Mahoney. To study the timeless appeal of pilgrimages, Mahoney visits England's Marian shrine at Walsingham and Lourdes in southern France, hikes the trail through the Pyrenees to Spain's Santiago de Compostela, spends two weeks in the Hindu holy city of Varanasi, travels to the Holy Land, and walks barefoot to St. Patrick's Purgatory on Ireland's Station Island. In this modern-day version of Chaucer's *Canterbury Tales*, on these six spiritual journeys, she encounters the boisterous and the believing, looking for "a preparation for death and a hedge against it."

ITALY THROUGH A WRITER'S EYES

Long before Frances Mayes whetted our appetites for vacations "under the Tuscan sun," writers couldn't resist putting pen to paper to capture the magic of Italy. Their work produced some of the best guidebooks you could find, books that help you appreciate the timeliness of Italian art and the country's rich history.

Start with John Ruskin. England's premier cultural critic in the mid-nineteenth century, he was so fascinated by Venetian art and architecture that he wrote a two-volume work on the subject, *The Stones of Venice.*

You don't have to read every word—a punishing prospect, unless the difference between doric and ionic columns is what turns you on. Instead, graze for ideas that will open your eyes to the cityscape.

Because of Ruskin, my husband and I discovered Torcello, an island seven miles and a universe away from the congestion in St. Mark's Square. Much more than an escape from the crowds, Torcello features a Romanesque church and a glimpse of Venice before its golden age. And the boat ride back, as sunset burnished the city in a soft light—for me, that's the moment that contains the magic of Venice.

In *The Stones of Florence,* American writer Mary McCarthy (*The Group* is the novel for which she's known) took a cue from Ruskin but produced a far more people-oriented guide, first published in 1959. She captures the sense of the place, whether she's talking about the city's history, its art, or the summer heat that turns the Arno Valley into a blazing furnace.

"The cruel tower of Palazzo Vecchio pierces the sky like a stone hypodermic needle," she writes. "The Duomo, outside, still astonishes by its bulk, which is altogether out of proportion with the narrow streets that lead up to it. It sits in the centre of Florence like a great hump of a snowy mountain deposited by some natural force, and it is, in fact, a kind of man-made mountain rising from the plain of the city and vying with the mountain of Fiesole, which can be seen in the distance."

A few travel books are written with such poetry and precision that they have no pull date, and this is one of them.

~ Ellen

5. *In the Company of the Courtesan* by Sarah Dunant. This novel about a Renaissance-era courtesan in Venice re-creates the time and place so effectively that it's almost like being there—after all, the city hasn't changed much. When the aging Fiammetta leaves war-torn Rome to peddle her charms up north, the dwarf Bucino is her eyes and ears. Their scheming sends him into the labyrinth of streets and piazzas that serve as a metaphor for the pair's intrigue. "Without a word being said, the fish swim into the net," Fiammetta tells Bucino. But sometimes the net gets snagged, too.

6. *The Places in Between* by Rory Stewart. If there's anything more quixotic than walking across Afghanistan in winter, it's being a westerner and making the hike right after 9/11. The sheer improbability of his two-month trek through an isolated mountain range makes his insights as remarkable as his survival. Key to both: The young Scot was no naïf. Steeped in the region's culture and history, he dodged danger to deliver a close-up, clear-eyed view of a society that's "an unpredictable composite of etiquette, humor, and extreme brutality." Ms. Manners meets mayhem.

7. *Nine Ways to Cross a River: Midstream Reflections on Swimming and Getting There From Here* by Akiko Busch. Swimming across the Hudson just before 9/11, Busch repeats the journey twice after the terrorist attack. She then crosses seven other American rivers. None are "what you would call a sport's challenge," she admits in this evocative account. The Delaware isn't wide. The Susquehanna is often shallow. The Connecticut is calm. The Monongahela, Mississippi, Ohio, and Current are all manageable. Why do it? "The river is what allows you to imagine that there are things that can go on forever."

8. *Crawfish Mountain: A Novel* by Ken Wells. Spider lilies, muskrats, and more politicians on the take than legs on a crawfish: Wells is back in his fictional Catahoula Bayou in Louisiana's wetlands. In this rowdy tale, set five years before Katrina hit, oilman Tom Huff wants to run an ecologically disastrous pipeline through the elevated marshland owned by Justin and Grace Pitre, a steamy Cajun couple. But the Pitres, who inherited Crawfish Mountain from Justin's Paw Paw, ain't selling. When you read Wells's descriptions of the view from the porch of their fishing cabin, you'll understand why.

9. *Unformed Landscape* by Peter Stamm. "Unformed landscape" doesn't only refer to the "day-wide empty snowscape" along the Norwegian coast where this haunting novel is set. Its protagonist is also formless. Kathrine, a divorcee and mother at twenty-five, has drifted into a loveless second marriage. When she catches her husband in a lie, she hops a freighter, traveling below the Arctic Circle to Stockholm and Paris. No, she doesn't find great wisdom. She simply returns to her icy homeland and finally shapes her life according to its rhythms and, more importantly, to her own.

10. *Trieste and the Meaning of Nowhere* by Jan Morris. Welsh writer Morris is known both for the sex-change operation that turned him into a woman and for her ability to evoke the sense of any place she goes. In Trieste, the faded port on the Adriatic where Morris was stationed during World War II, she finds a drabness, a drifting quality attributed to the passing of its glory days as an imperial city and Mitteleuropa melting pot. "Melancholy is Trieste's chief rapture," Morris writes. "Trieste makes one ask sad questions of oneself. What am I here for? Where am I going?"

THAT MAKE YOU LAUGH

1. *God Bless You, Dr. Kevorkian* by Kurt Vonnegut. These snippets are based on ninety-second spots Vonnegut, who died in 2007, did for public radio in the '90s. As a "reporter of the afterlife," he underwent (wink, wink) "controlled near-death experiences" under the supervision of Jack Kevorkian, traveling round-trip to the Pearly Gates to interview the dead, from John Brown (still "a-molderin'") to the first American to cross the Alps in a hot-air balloon ("That was heaven, and I was still alive"). Oh, and to forestall your own demise, Vonnegut advises: "Use sunscreen!"

2. *The Third Policeman* by Flann O'Brien. Gaelic-speaking O'Brien (born Brian O'Nuallain) loved to poke fun at his native soil. In this comic novel, a man dies but doesn't realize he's dead because the corner of Hell he finds himself in, a rural police precinct, looks so much like Ireland. Brace yourself for high satire and groan-producing puns, not to mention all-out goofiness. The policemen are confiscating bicycles because they believe, thanks to the movement of molecules, that people who ride them are becoming part bicycle. O'Brien died on April Fools' Day in 1966.

3. *You Can Lead a Politician to Water, But You Can't Make Him Think: Ten Commandments for Texas Politics* by Kinky Friedman. Following in the footsteps of celebrity guvs Arnold Schwarzenegger and Jesse Ventura, in 2006 Jewish cowboy and political wiseguy Friedman threw his "ten-gallon yarmulke" in the ring and ran for the top job in Texas. He lost, but he continues to rail against the system in this folksy, even-handed, and profane take on politics. The World According to Kinky: "Politics is the only field in which the more experience you have, the worse you get."

4. *The Late Bloomer's Revolution: A Memoir* by Amy Cohen. This sitcom writer and dating columnist has drowned her sorrows in so much pound cake and cream puffs that she should be as wide as she is tall. Hmmm. Then how could the attractive woman pictured on the jacket be the same anguished, acne-drenched, "emotionally incontinent" loser in love she describes in her book? Chalk up the discrepancy to her comic gifts mixed with her taste for men "who felt about settling down the way cats feel about being thrown into a full bathtub." It's a perfect recipe.

5. *My Latest Grievance* by Elinor Lipman. Just like the stuffy English gent, the PC crowd is ripe for satire because it's so easy to recognize. Lipman plays this for laughs with the Hatches, faculty members who have raised their only child in the dorm and their drab, intellectually superior world of high ideals. But "I wanted to be cool," narrator Frederica recalls. When her dad's glamorous ex shows up on campus, Frederica finds a new role model. There's nothing wrong with high-mindedness, of course, but sometimes the other guy's moccasins aren't nearly as fun to occupy as a pair of three-inch heels.

6. *The Lecturer's Tale* by James Hynes. Novelists as diverse as Evelyn Waugh and Jane Smiley have found the absurdity in academia. But Hynes goes beyond satire into supreme wackiness through his fictional protagonist Nelson Humboldt, low man on the English department pole at the fictional University of the Midwest. The same day Nelson is fired, a freak accident severs his finger. Reattached, the finger confers magic powers that work wonders among the backbiting, brown-nosing profs. The whole finger thing plays off Nelson's remark that "a man's reach should exceed his grasp."

7. *Bowl of Cherries* by Millard Kaufman. You gotta love an author who at ninety writes a funny first novel. In this bawdy coming-of-age tale, Kaufmann, the cocreator of Mr. Magoo, looks clear-eyed at adolescent angst through fourteen-year-old Judd Breslau. The setting shifts from a Colorado horse ranch to a porn studio under the Brooklyn Bridge to an Iraqi jail cell where Breslau awaits his execution. Breslau narrates his story using a self-important, overblown prose you'd expect from a precocious college-drop out (from Yale, no less), but with a modern, ironic twist. Think Holden Caulfield channeling Stephen Colbert.

8. *The Position* by Meg Wolitzer. The basic agreement between most parents and their offspring is that Mom and Dad won't talk about their sex lives, and the kids won't ask. That's a problem for the Mellow family in this satiric novel that makes fun of the American view of sex: Parental fame and fortune rest on the highly personal best seller *Pleasuring: One Couple's Journey to Ful-fillment,* which, to say the least, takes away the mystery for their four children. Thirty years later, the couple is divorced, the kids are struggling with their legacy, and you get the sense that sex manuals bare all but leave something out.

9. *Get Your Tongue Out of My Mouth, I'm Kissing You Good-bye* by Cynthia Heimel. Heimel's titles (*If You Can't Live Without Me, Why Aren't You Dead Yet?!* and *If You Leave Me, Can I Come Too?*) aren't the only thing that's funny about her books. In her essays, the former *Playboy* columnist (she apparently was dropped be-cause editors feared her ballsy comments were putting off male readers) takes on the battle between the sexes with mordant wit.

Her most famous line (a variation on Gloria Steinem's favorite ditty): "Women need men like a fish needs a net."

10. *The Pirates! In an Adventure With Scientists, The Pirates! In an Adventure With Ahab,* and *The Pirates! In an Adventure With Communists* by Gideon Defoe. These loopy exploits of Pirate Captain and his pirates ("the pirate with a nut allergy," "the pirate with gout") make Johnny Depp's Captain Jack Sparrow look positively sane. Whether attacking Darwin's *Beagle,* searching for Melville's white whale, teaming up with Karl Marx and Friedrich Engels, or arguing over "the best bit of being a pirate" (the looting? the doubloons? the cutlasses?), it's pure swash-buckling lunacy.

THAT ARE REAL KILLERS

1. *In Cold Blood* by Truman Capote. "Death, brutal and without apparent motive": That was the message delivered from church pulpits and by radio after two graduates of the Kansas State Penitentiary murdered four members of a farm family in 1959. Capote plucked the story from the headlines and re-created it as part of the emerging form called literary journalism. His method puts you inside the heads of two psychopaths and helps you appreciate how random and thoughtless their actions were. There's nothing consoling about the story, just a writing tour de force.

2. *The Alienist* by Caleb Carr. In this atmospheric novel set in nineteenth-century New York, young male prostitutes are being murdered. The city's police commissioner, none other than Theodore Roosevelt, seeks the help of two people to catch the serial killer: Dr. Laszio Kreizler, an alienist (today's criminal psychologist), and John Schuyler Moore, a *New York Times* crime reporter (who narrates this heart-pounding tale). Interested in why someone kills, Kreizler tests out his theories of criminal profiling, the early signs of an emerging forensic science: "We're all still running . . . running away from the darkness we know to lie behind so many tranquil household doors."

3. *The Devil in the White City: Murder, Magic, and Madness at the Fair That Changed America* by Erik Larson. The killer in *The Alienist* was an invention. But in 1893 a real killer was claiming multiple victims: not prostitutes but dozens of unsuspecting women tourists. While Daniel Burnham, a visionary architect, was building the "white city" of that year's world's fair, H. H. Holmes was luring victims to his hotel. Holmes later admitted to killing twenty-eight, but recovered human parts indicate he killed more than two hundred. Says Larson in this gripping account: "This was Chicago, on the eve of the greatest fair in history."

4. *Strange Piece of Paradise* by Terri Jentz. Decades after the fact, Jentz revisits the cross-country summer biking trip that ended abruptly when a man attacked her and a friend with an axe while they were camping in Oregon's high desert. Both survived, but Jentz's account is more about the emotional aftermath. She identifies her likely attacker as a guy with a hot fist for his girlfriends.

"If I, of all people, had found myself linked to these battered women through one violent man," she writes, "how prevalent this male violence against women must be—and what a long shadow it surely casts on the lives of all women."

5. *Asylum* by Patrick McGrath. This haunting novel about a woman who goes over the edge brings to mind the famous line from Scottish psychiatrist R. D. Laing: "Insanity is a sane response to an insane world." Dominated by her husband, a shrink who runs the mental hospital where they live, Stella Raphael escapes into a doomed affair with a patient. Her story is told by one of her husband's colleagues, whose own agenda slowly emerges in his telling of the tale. "Romantic women," he reflects, "they never think of the damage they do in their blind pursuit of intense experience."

6. *Under the Banner of Heaven* by Jon Krakauer. The murder of a former beauty queen and her baby daughter is Krakauer's vehicle for exploring homegrown religious zealotry and what one Mormon historian describes as "the continued spread of unauthorized polygamy among the Latter-day Saints during the last seventy-five years, despite the concerted efforts of Church leaders to stop it." The killers are the woman's brothers-in-law, who decide she's too uppity. In Krakauer's mind, polygamy and this murder both involve a vicious assault on women's rights and personhood.

7. *The Suspicions of Mr. Whicher: A Shocking Murder and the Undoing of a Great Victorian Detective* by Kate Summerscale. Study

of the unconscious mind was in its infancy in 1860, when Jack Whicher, "the prince of detectives" at Scotland Yard, was sent to investigate the murder of three-year-old Saville Kent. Pursuing his hunch that the blond boy's sixteen-year-old half sister was the killer, he failed to prove his case and his career was ruined. Summerscale's deep look into the truth and consequences of this real-life sensation uncovers family secrets and the timeless taste for scandal.

8. *Shadow Country* by Peter Matthiessen. E. J. Watson, a real-life planter in the Everglades of frontier Florida, was a brutal man. But why did his neighbors gang up and pump thirty-three rounds of ammo into him? Matthiessen explores that question in this fictional retelling, a combination of his previous three novels about the man known as Bloody Watson. Giving voice to an era when racial hatred was virulent and violence easy, he even lets Watson have his say: "Whenever someone threatens to tell tales on me, get me into trouble, a taste of iron comes into my mouth."

9. *While They Slept: An Inquiry Into the Murder of a Family* by Kathryn Harrison. "It's an addiction, true crime, easy to satisfy," Harrison begins, tracing her own fixation for the genre to the psychological damage caused by her father's sexual abuse. Her fascination draws her to the aftermath of a 1984 triple murder in which a brother killed his parents and one of his sisters, while another sister in the household at the same time was left unscathed. He's doing time, but she is more traumatized. Such unthinkable experiences "have a long half-life," Harrison notes. "People don't recover from them so much as manage their effects."

10. *The Stranger Beside Me* by Ann Rule. When Rule first wrote in 1980 about Ted Bundy, she underscored this chilling fact about serial killers: They could be anybody. She had met Bundy, who was executed in 1989, while both were manning a Seattle suicide hotline in 1971. At first, she didn't believe he was capable of such horrors. In her twentieth-anniversary update of her book on the notorious murderer, she speculates that his killing spree may have begun when he was fourteen. Eight-year-old Ann Marie Burr, who lived on Bundy's newspaper route, disappeared and has never been found.

THAT CELEBRATE THE DICK

1. *Hardboiled and High Heeled: The Woman Detective in Popular Culture* by Linda Mizejewski. "Whatsa matter," Kathleen Turner smirks in the 1991 movie *V. I. Warshawski,* based on Sara Paretsky's female detective, "haven't you ever seen a female dick?" Now, hardboiled heroines are everywhere, says Mizejewski in this study of their images in movies, television, and books. But Paretsky's creation along with Sue Grafton's alphabet-series star Kinsey Millhone, who first appeared in 1982, led the way: "loners, wise about taking care of themselves, skilled with a gun and ready to use it if necessary."

2. *The Tin Roof Blowdown: A Dave Robicheaux Novel* by James Lee Burke. The above description also fits Cajun ex-cop Dave

Robicheaux, one of our favorite male dicks. Here, through the brooding Robicheaux who works out of New Orleans, Burke vents his rage against the incompetence that followed Katrina. After two looters are shot breaking into the home of a mobster in the aftermath of the storm, Robicheaux goes out looking for their surviving accomplice. The search is a heartbreaking journey through the greed and violence of a drowned city.

3. *Death in Holy Orders* (**Adam Dalgliesh Mystery Series**) by P. D. James. In this series James offers another irresistible male detective: the poetry-reading Adam Dalgliesh, from Scotland Yard. Here, Dalgliesh's investigation takes him to a theological college on the coast of East Anglia. The isolated setting evokes the Golden Age of British cozies, when suspects were trapped in a manor house as bodies piled up. But don't expect the butler in the library with the wrench à la the game of Clue. James, specializing in psychologically complex characters, elevates the mystery genre to a fine art.

4. *The Miracle at Speedy Motors* (**No. 1 Ladies Detective Series**) by Alexander McCall Smith. Speaking of powerful settings, this lighthearted series transports you to Bostwana, where Precious Ramotswe, a full-figured lady detective, tries "to help people with problems in their lives." Here, "Mma" Ramotswe, who speaks in a lilting African English, is tracking down an adopted woman's family. She's also trying to persuade her esteemed husband, Mr. J. L. B. Matekoni, who works at Speedy Motors, that he is in the thrall of a quack. Of course, all the while, pausing to sip her bush tea.

5. *The Corpse Had a Familiar Face: Covering Miami, America's Hottest Beat* by Edna Buchanan. A hard-nosed *Miami Herald* crime reporter, Buchanan quit journalism to write a mystery series starring the hard-nosed Brit Montero, a crime reporter for the *Miami News*. But as these true-crime stories, written and published when Buchanan was still a journalist, show, fiction has nothing on reality. Her goal at the *Herald*: "To write a lead that will cause a reader at his breakfast table to spit up his coffee, clutch at his heart, and shout, 'My God, Martha, did you read this?'"

6. *Case Histories* by Kate Atkinson. "'Closure,' that was what they called it. It sounded so Californian." With the seen-it-all scorn of a veteran private eye, Atkinson's fictional British detective, Jackson Brodie, takes on three seemingly unconnected cold cases: a child's disappearance, a young woman's murder, a husband axed to death by his wife. As each mystery is solved, the author slyly underscores the power of empathy and the interconnectedness of all beings. Brodie's tip for aspiring private investigators: There's always a Chatty Cathy or Blabby Barbara the police forgot to interview.

7. *The Name of the Rose* by Umberto Eco. Despite its reputation as a novel left on coffee tables unread, this medieval mystery is an approachable rumination on faith and laughter. Set in the library of an Italian monastery headed by Jorge of Borgos (a nod to Argentinian writer Jorge Borges), the tale begins with a murder. Brother William of Baskerville (named after Arthur Conan Doyle's hounds) arrives to investigate. As more bodies turn up, remember the wisdom handed down by that other fourteenth-century friar, William of Ockham: The simplest answer is best.

8. *Of Blood and Sorrow* (A Tamara Hayle Mystery) by Valerie Wilson Wesley. After Lilah Love—a woman with "a pretty, nut brown face and a mop of fake red hair that screamed twenty-dollar hooker"—walks into Tamara Hayle's detective agency, trouble and a mounting body count are not far behind. Blackboard-bestseller Wesley's sleuth, a single mom raising a teenage son, is sassy and smart, and so is Wesley's series, set at the intersection between those who've made it and those still struggling on the mean streets of Newark.

9. *The Blood Spilt* by Asa Larsson. Dark deeds take place in a land of nearly constant light in Larsson's follow-up to her debut *Sun Storm*. Junior lawyer Rebecka Martinsson and inspector Anna-Maria Mella are thrown together again after a woman activist priest is brutally murdered in the northernmost Swedish town of Kiruna. The plot keeps you guessing. But as with Ruth Rendell's psychological thrillers, Larsson's probe into the mind of the killer is what fascinates most. As the unnamed murderer says in the chilling opening scene: "I am racing into the far country that is madness."

10. *Masterpieces in Miniature: The Detectives—Stories by Agatha Christie* by Agatha Christie. These thirty-nine short stories by the undisputed queen of crime feature Christie's most popular detectives: Parker Pyne, a statistician who peddles happiness to his clients; Harley Quin, a supernatural figure working miracles; Hercule Poirot, the Belgian private eye famous for his "little gray cells"; and (our favorite) Miss Jane Marple, the spinster who solves crimes in St. Mary's Mead. Is Marple "the last word in sleuths"? No, she demurs, "Nothing of the kind. It's just that living in a village as I do, one gets to know so much about human nature."

THAT MAKE 10 FEEL ROYAL

1. *The Lady Elizabeth* by Alison Weir. Weir and Philippa Gregory are the two biggest names in historical fiction about the Tudors. Exhibit A: this novel, in which Weir paints England's Elizabeth I during the perilous years before she ascends to the throne. Her precocious intelligence and survival instincts set the stage for success even as half-sister Mary blunders her way to the top. The Virgin Queen is no such thing in this version of her life—a bit of poetic license, Weir admits—but the proof is in the pudding when it comes to her knack for political intrigue.

2. *Elizabeth & Mary: Cousins, Rivals, Queens* by Jane Dunn. Bess is back! (See above.) In this version, biographer Dunn's side-by-side portrait exposes the suspicious times, contrasting personalities, and a reversal of fortune worthy of a Greek tragedy. In 1558, when the book opens, Mary Queen of Scots seems set for life, wedding a French prince and knitting together England's enemies, France and Scotland. Poor cuz Elizabeth! She's just one step ahead of the axe. Luck helped, but wits made the big difference between who ended up ruling the waves and who lost her head.

3. *Murder of a Medici Princess* by Caroline P. Murphy. Daddy's girl has a problem when Daddy dies, at least if she's a Medici. Isabella, member of the Florentine family whose taste for art fueled the Italian Renaissance, was a high-spirited sixteenth-century woman with a powerful and "instinctively paternal" papa. (One should hope: His wife gave him eleven children.) Her estranged hubby and resentful brother weren't so indulgent. Her father inadvertently laid the trap: Having grown up with immense privilege, Isabella didn't know how to play defense.

4. *Christina Queen of Sweden: The Restless Life of a European Eccentric* by Veronica Buckley. An early feminist who often wore men's attire, Christina wasn't queen of Lutheran Sweden for long. In 1654, at twenty-eight, she abdicated, supposedly to convert to Catholicism. The young queen moved to Italy, not drawn by religion, says biographer Buckley, but by a love of art and a desire for independence. "Christina's world was a crossroads world, where God still ruled but men had begun to doubt. She herself would stand at many crossroads, of religion and power, of science and society and sex."

5. *Versailles: A Novel* by Kathryn Davis. Let them eat cake? Hardly. This Marie Antoinette, imagined from the inside, has the fey, openhearted personality of a valley girl. She shows up to marry her initially impotent king, wallows in the gilt and grandeur of court life, and finally bears the heirs who will never serve France. It's the stupidity of out-of-touch aristocrats, not Antoinette, that creates mud-spattered crowds shouting for bread. But the queen becomes their bête noire. Finally, she realizes: "Something that has held for hundreds of years is blowing apart." Too late, my pretty, too late.

6. *Catherine the Great: Love, Sex and Power* by Virginia Rounding. Forget the idea that she had sex with a horse: pure fiction, of course! Yet the rumor suggests what a passionate woman Catherine was, in the boudoir and as advocate for Mother Russia. German-born, she ascended the throne after her emperor husband was assassinated in 1762. Although this bio can't confirm she did him in, she hated him enough to skip the funeral. A woman who was "not given to wasting time or energy indulging in useless re-grets," she used reason and ruthlessness to complete work started by that other Great, Peter.

7. *Empress Orchid* by Anchee Min. In the nineteenth century, imperial China was collapsing. But it was a long, slow death interrupted by a cattle call for concubines that in this novel takes the humble teenager Orchid out of poverty and into the shadowy depths of the Forbidden City. Well, if you've gotten this far, why hesitate? Orchid allies herself with a clever eunuch and charms the emperor. When she gets the prize—a bun in the oven—she starts fighting for two. Min's fictional tale, based on a woman who redefined the term *imperious*, re-creates a world in which extreme luxury coexisted with breathtaking cruelty.

8. *The Reluctant Empress: A Biography of Empress Elisabeth of Austria* by Brigitte Hamann. The shy Bavarian beauty nicknamed

Sisi hardly knew what she was up against when she agreed to marry her cousin, Austrian emperor Franz Joseph I, in 1853. Too high-strung for the gossip and pressures of court life in Vienna, she retreated to anorexia, starving herself and working out like a gymnast to maintain her nineteen-inch waist. Hamann's bio captures the whole scene: the hapless Franz Joseph, the rejected son Rudolph (who died mysteriously), and the sense of yet another empire in decline.

9. *Leap of Faith: Memoirs of an Unexpected Life* by Queen Noor. Lisa Halaby's story will do nothing to discourage American girls' dreams of royalty. In 1978, at age twenty-six, she became Queen Noor (Arabic for "light") when she married Jordan's forty-one-year-old King Hussein. In this memoir she describes her private and public life with the monarch who became the father of her four children. Hussein, who died in 1999, was known as a broker of peace in the Arab world. This book honors that legacy by putting a human face on an area little understood by most Americans.

10. *The Diana Chronicles* by Tina Brown. Who better to weigh in on the world's most famous royal (or, at least, the most photographed) than tough-skinned magazine maven Tina Brown, who turned dish into a literary art form? She provides plenty of juicy insider details chronicling Diana's troubled life and, blessedly, goes beyond the usual clichés about the Princess of Wales: chic and compassionate, yes, but also manipulative and vindictive. Yet even the cynical Brown is moved by this beautiful woman and her magical sweetness. "Diana's smile was a laser that went straight to the heart."

THAT WILL BREAK YOUR HEART

1. *The Remains of the Day* by Kazuo Ishiguro. In this novel, an aging English butler motors cross country to convince a former housekeeper to return to service. As he reminisces about their time together just before World War II, you realize the depth of his delusion about his pro-Nazi employer. You also realize, before he does, his real feelings for Miss Keaton, now Mrs. Benn. This preknowledge is lost in the movie version, which uses an impersonal voiceover to tell the story. In the novel, Stevens speaks directly with stiff upper lip. Listen closely: You'll hear the sound of his shattered heart.

2. *The Notebook* by Nicholas Sparks. When this novel opens with an old man reading a story to an Alzheimer's patient, you already know you're in for a good cry. You just don't know if they will be tears of joy or sorrow. The story, whose film version is also a tearjerker, is about lovesick teenagers from New Bern, North Carolina; World War II and purposely mislaid letters; moving away and moving up, but never really moving on. Oh, and house restoration. When the old man closes up the notebook, be prepared: The floodgates will open and, omigod, they are tears of sorrow *and* joy.

3. *We Wish to Inform You That Tomorrow We Will be Killed With Our Families: Stories from Rwanda* by Philip Gourevitch. In this

heartbreaking reportage about the 1994 hundred-day-long mas-
sacre in Rwanda that left more than 800,000 dead, you'll weep for
both sides of such madness. Says Gourevitch: "Every Rwandan I
spoke with seemed to have a favorite, unanswerable question."
For Laurent Nkongoli, a Tutsi lawyer, it was how so many Tutsis
had allowed themselves to be killed. For Francois Xavier Nku-
runziza, half Hutu and half Tutsi, it was how so many Hutus had
allowed themselves to kill.

4. *Flowers for Algernon* by Daniel Keyes. This 1966 Nebula
Award–winning novel is told in the voice of Charlie Gordon, I.Q.
68. After undergoing a brain enhancement operation that already
has worked wonders on the lab mouse named Algernon, Gordon
writes "progris riports" that become more and more literate but
also more aware of the cruelties of life as the operation turns him
(and Algernon) into geniuses. But it doesn't take a genius to realize that this upward trend is doomed, and as Gordon watches the
mouse deteriorate, you ache when you realize he is about to lose
himself again.

5. *The Curious Incident of the Dog in the Night-Time* by Mark
Haddon. "I think prime numbers are like life. They are very
logical but you could never work out the rules, even if you
spent all your time thinking about them." Welcome to the
world of Christopher John Francis Boone, an autistic boy who
has a normal IQ but is color-blind to emotions. After he finds a
dead dog in the neighbor's yard, he takes you along while he
solves the mystery. His investigation pulls the lid off a bunch of

secrets, revelations made sadder because you see what's unfolding when he can't.

6. *Talk Before Sleep* by Elizabeth Berg. Ruth is dying of breast cancer, but this novel is not so much about how she copes as it is about how her female friends do. They bring her ice cream and lobster, fend off her heartless ex-husband and, reluctantly, let her go when she decides to spend her last days with her brother in Florida. When Ann, the novel's narrator, finally gets the call that her friend is gone, she hangs up and immediately makes another call. Halfway through dialing, she realizes whom she's calling: "Ruth, to tell her she died."

7. *Eavesdropping: A Memoir of Blindness and Listening* by Stephen Kuusisto. In this book and his earlier one, *The Planet of the Blind,* poet and teacher Kuusisto describes how accepting that he can't see opened up his world. An intense relationship with music started early, when sad lyrics had his name on them: "I was a student of loneliness." Recalling the splashing oars and musty smells in Venice, he responds to the stupid woman who wonders why the blind travel when they can't see the places they go. His world may be dark, but it's full of sound, feeling, and love.

8. *Atonement* by Ian McEwan. Cecilia is a snob from the British upper classes. Robbie's the cleaning lady's son whose Cambridge education was paid for by Cecilia's admiring father. As their yearning for each other bursts into view, thirteen-year-old

Briony enters stage left, rewriting their romance to push Robbie out. This prize-winning novel testifies to the kind of love that endures all things and makes you weep at the sacrifices it engenders. "Realistically, there had to be a choice—you or them," Cecilia writes to Robbie. "You are my dearest one, my reason for life."

9. *The Lost: A Search for Six of Six Million* by Daniel Mendelsohn. Am I my brother's keeper? It's a question at least as old as the Hebrew Bible, and one asked anew in Mendelsohn's multifaceted memoir. When his Jewish aunts burst into tears over his resemblance to a lost uncle, Mendelsohn can't shake the ghost of that man and five other Polish relatives who died in the Holocaust. His memoir weaves together their stories with a Talmudic meditation on Scripture and a reflection on the meaning of family ties, putting a face—six, in fact—on the millions who perished in Hitler's genocide.

10. *The Known World* by Edward P. Jones. As this novel wrenchingly demonstrates, American slavery was truly a house of mirrors. William Robbins, the most powerful white slave owner in Manchester County, Virginia, is desperately in love with a black woman. Henry Townsend, who is black, is also a slave owner (yes, that historically did occur) in the same county. Townsend got his taste for owning human property from Robbins, his ex-master, who helped him purchase his first slave. As Moses, one of those slaves, says when he finds out he's owned by a black man: "Was God even up there attending to business anymore?"

BOOKS ABOUT BOOKS

1. *The Library at Night* by Alberto Manguel. Manguel probes the magic and mystery of libraries, using black-and-white photos to enhance the spell, in this stroll through both his own and famous book repositories through history. Inspired by Diderot and Dewey, libraries catalogue the ever-expanding reach of human thought and discovery, while the books within have a life of their own. "Left to their own devices, they assemble in unexpected formations," Manguel writes. "A library is not only a place of both order and chaos; it is also the realm of chance."

2. *Writing in an Age of Silence* by Sara Paretsky. Famed crime writer Paretsky merges political manifesto and memoir here, offering an impassioned plea for equal opportunity—in the world, and in book publishing. With roots in rural Kansas and a girlhood built on *Little Women* and traditional women's roles, Paretsky jumped ship to feminist activism in her college years and later invented her girl detective partly to address issues of class and wealth. V. I. Warshawski "does not try to save the world," she explains. "But, in her own small milieu, she tries, as Lincoln did, to 'bind up . . . wounds.'"

3. *The Well of Lost Plots: A Thursday Next Novel* by Jasper Fforde. In this outing of the imaginative series where real people and book characters collide within the pages of books, Special Ops Thursday

Next takes up residence in a lousy unpublished crime thriller named *Caversham Heights.* (The novel has "a pace so slow that snails pass it in the night.") Next, part of a group charged with saving world lit, is pregnant and needs a break. But living in a novel, she discovers, has dangers (including murder) as well as more minor drawbacks. "There was no TV . . . unless called for in the narrative."

4. *An Arsonist's Guide to Writers' Homes in New England: A Novel* by Brock Clarke. This novel is the oddest tour you'll ever get of New England literature. After accidentally burning down Emily Dickinson's house in Amherst, Massachusetts (and killing two people), for which he served a ten-year sentence, narrator Sam Pulsifer is turning his life around. But when the houses of Edward Bellamy, Mark Twain, Edith Wharton, and Robert Frost are torched, he becomes the suspect. No wonder he describes himself as a bumbler: "Would even sad-sack Ethan Frome look at me and feel lucky?"

5. *The Lie That Tells a Truth: A Guide to Writing Fiction* by John Dufresne. You don't have to be writing a novel to appreciate this guide to the craft. A writing teacher and author of compelling fiction himself, Dufresne (*Louisiana Power and Light* and *Deep in the Shade of Paradise*) demystifies the writing process for everyone. For writers in need of a plot, he provides one that Russian author Anton Chekov sketched out but never used. For readers, he offers a fascinating behind-the-scenes look at just how the sausage of fiction is made.

6. *How to Read Literature Like a Professor: A Lively and Entertaining Guide to Reading Between the Lines* by Thomas C. Foster. How do you get the most out of reading literature? "Same way you get to Carnegie Hall," says the learned professor. "Practice." We're cool with that: Reading a lot and making connections is key. But so is appreciating symbolic language—spring as a time of renewal, and ghosts as something more than ghosts. As for the X-rated parts, this, too, is usually a stand-in for something else. In this post-Freudian era, how could it be just about the sex?

7. *Written Lives* by Javier Marias. Here's the perfect "bathroom book" for literary snobs. These "snippets" focus on famous writers' lives, with a potpourri of personal details and death scenes delivered with insouciance and wit. James Joyce, who "was always convinced of the extreme importance of his work, even before it existed," was the dinner partner from hell. ("Yes," "no," or silence.) Thomas Mann, he of furrowed brow, "really believed that he did not take himself seriously." And Isak Dinesen, no pointy head, had but one request when she came to America: to meet Marilyn Monroe.

8. *The McSweeney's Joke Book of Book Jokes* by McSweeney's. The front and back covers of this book have been switched, the first indication that literature is about to be turned on its ear. These short essays from the hip San Francisco publisher mix classics with pop culture, with very funny results. Imagine Jane Eyre running for president and being interviewed by MSNBC's Chris Matthews. Or the feedback Homer would get if he joined a writing workshop. ("Excellent word economy, as usual.") The shortest offering is "Holden Caulfield Gives the Commencement Speech to a High School": "You're all a bunch of goddam phonies."

9. *Classics for Pleasure* by Michael Dirda. No jokes here. Just the intelligence of ace critic Dirda's short essays on writers from Sappho to Eudora Welty (stories "as mysterious, alluring and beautiful as any in our literature"), from Lucian to H. P. Lovecraft, creator of the creepiest fiction since Poe. Along the way some surprises: Who would have thunk a gloomy Gus like existential philosopher Soren Kierkegaard could compose the *Diary of a Seducer*? Or that Daphne du Maurier of *Rebecca* fame also wrote the fable that would become an Alfred Hitchcock classic, *The Birds*?

10. *Literacy and Longing in L.A.* by Jennifer Kaufman and Karen Mack. When Dora, named for Eudora Welty, is depressed (about soon-to-be exes), she goes on a book binge (doesn't everyone?), holing herself up for days with Emily, Sylvia, and F. Scott until her sister, Virginia, named for guess who, coaxes her back to the real world. No wonder she falls for Fred, the bookstore hottie. But guys who quote Cicero and Proust are not often the real thing, she learns. This novel gives you enough reading material for your own marathon, zonked-out literary bender.

THE BOOK BABES COULDN'T LIVE WITHOUT

Ellen:

1. *Emotional Intelligence: Why It Can Matter More Than I.Q.* by Daniel Goleman. Being smart, American-style, means being an achiever. That's why Goleman's book, first published in the mid-

'90s, broke new ground by emphasizing the need for empathy, both as a personal asset and a cultural necessity. As the mother of two growing sons, I took this message to heart, because boys in particular are under pressure to believe winning isn't the thing, it's the only thing. Goleman earns five stars for elevating the status of people who play well with others: They're not just smart. They're emotionally intelligent.

2. *Disturbances in the Field* by Lynne Sharon Schwartz. More from a mom's point of view: What is a mother's greatest nightmare? Losing one of her children, of course. Try two, and you've hit the key to this novel about grief and what it does to a well-ordered life. The fictional Lydia Rowe is a pianist with an artist husband and an urbane life in Manhattan. Then—*kebam!* The bottom falls out. "There is an essential and profound strangeness about being a mother that is rarely spoken of," Schwartz writes. Her story goes to the heart of what making a family is all about.

3. *A Fine Balance* by Rohinton Mistry. Blood ties are important, but so are the kind cobbled together out of circumstance. Mistry's fiction masterpiece, set in India during the 1970s, unveils the strength and terror of Indira Gandhi's rule from the bottom up. His four characters—a college student, a seamstress, a tailor, and his nephew—band together and have a chance of finding that "fine balance between hope and despair" to which the title alludes. Their fate reminded me of the fine balance between the comfortable life I've had and its opposite. The most insidious aspect about poverty is the loss of hope.

4. *The Life You Save May Be Your Own: An American Pilgrimage* by Paul Elie. This is one of those loose-limbed books that's hard to define: Neither traditional biography nor history, it's more of a rumination on four famous Catholics from the twentieth century—Dorothy Day, Flannery O'Connor, Thomas Merton, and Walker Percy—and their lifelong pilgrimages toward spiritual wholeness through action and art. Although not Catholic, I find in each of their stories a sense of my ongoing struggle to be a person of faith and make it evident in my life.

5. *Homestead* by Rosina Lippi. This novel about how the twentieth century flowed through one Austrian village sits on a packed shelf with related books such as Bernhard Schlink's *The Reader,* Rachel Seiffert's *The Dark Room,* and Ron Rosenbaum's *Explaining Hitler.* Lippi's story captures the culture in a high mountain setting worthy of *Heidi.* Told through the lives of various local women, it reminds me of the devastation of two world wars that still can be seen on church plaques honoring the dead in nearly every German town.

Margo:

1. *If on a Winter's Night a Traveler* by Italo Calvino. In every other chapter of this novel, another story begins, written in yet another literary style. They are story fragments that have been inserted in books bought by the Reader and the Other Reader in a diabolical plot to subvert reading. But, of course, reading just stimulates more reading in this imaginative story that celebrates the joy of cracking open a new book: "Adjust the light so you won't strain your eyes. Do it now, because once you're absorbed in reading, there will be no budging you."

2. *New Orleans, Mon Amour: Twenty Years of Writing From the City* by Andrei Codrescu. In 1982, Codrescu (the NPR commentator with the Romanian vowels) went to visit writer Philip Herter in New Orleans for Mardi Gras and never really left. This collection of essays is haunting, not surprising coming from a city with so many ghosts afoot. Codrescu, my colleague at the *Baltimore Sun* in the early '80s, reports the facts, but his are filtered through a poet's eyes. Arriving in Louisiana: "Time itself underwent a subtle but decisive transformation. I felt tropical, fragrant, and observant."

3. *Out Stealing Horses* by Per Petterson. My taste in novels vacillates between sprawling epics à la Salman Rushdie's *Midnight's Children* and spare gems like Jim Crace's *Being Dead*. Petterson's falls into the latter category, with the added bonus of being set in Scandinavia, the home of my mother's ancestors. A coming-of-age tale, a mystery, and a history lesson, it's told in the voice of an old Norwegian man whose meeting with a neighbor triggers a memory of the day when he teetered between the warmth of childhood and the icy winter of growing up.

4. *Team of Rivals: The Political Genius of Abraham Lincoln* by Doris Kearns Goodwin. Politics are my passion, but no one can break my heart faster than a politician. Here, Goodwin restores my faith: not all of them are power-hungry partisans. "A house divided against itself cannot stand," Lincoln had said, referring to

the existence of slave and free states. Goodwin's eloquently describes how "the prairie lawyer from Springfield" managed to unite rather than divide by reaching out to the three men who were his rivals in the race for the presidency and turning them into allies. It's a lesson for all times.

5. *Good Poems for Hard Times* selected and introduced by Garrison Keillor. Minnesotan Keillor, neighbor to my native Wisconsin, represents the best of the Midwest, combining book learnin' and common sense. "What your life can be, lived bravely and independently, you can discover in poetry," he says in the introduction to this collection, which includes poems from Virginia Hamilton Adair to Walt Whitman. As Rita Dove says in "Dawn Revisited": "The whole sky is yours / to write on, blown open / to a blank page. Come on, / shake a leg! You'll never know / who's down there, frying those eggs, / if you don't get up and see."

Index

Index

Index

Index

Index